The Year of the Monkey
and other plays

Claire Dowie is a writer/performer/poet/comedian, and pioneer of 'stand-up theatre'. After starting out on the 'alternative' comedy circuit, she switched to stand-up comedy and to writing plays 'when the punchlines ran out'. Her first major work, *Adult Child/Dead Child*, won a Time Out Award in 1988. Other works include *Why is John Lennon Wearing a Skirt?*, *Easy Access (For the Boys)*, *All Over Lovely* (all available from Methuen), *Came Out, It Rained, Went Back In Again*, for BBC2's City Shorts season, *Kevin* for Central Children's Television, and *From the Bottom of a Well* and *The Barnes Originals* (both for BBC radio and both performed by Stephen Moore). *Designs for Living* was produced by Ruby Tuesday for the Drill Hall, London, in April 2001. For further information on Claire Dowie's work, see her official website at www.geocities.com/clairedowie_2000.

The Year of the Monkey
Designs for Living
Sodom

Claire Dowie

Methuen Drama

Published by Methuen 2001

1 3 5 7 9 10 8 6 4 2

First published in 2001 by Methuen Publishing Limited
215 Vauxhall Bridge Road, London SW1V 1EJ

Methuen Publishing Limited Reg. No. 3543167

ISBN 0 413 76180 0

Typeset by SX Composing DTP, Rayleigh, Essex
Printed and bound in Great Britain by
Cox & Wyman Ltd, Reading, Berkshire

Contents

The Year of the Monkey

Bonfire Night
Arsehammers
Allotments
The Year of the Monkey

Bonfire Night

If you hear a loud bang on bonfire night do you think it's a firework . . . or a gun going off?

I'll get Dad sorted and leave about five. Sandwiches and milk, that should do him, he knows the arrangement, bonfire-night-is-my-night-off! I'll put him a fresh jug of water – but I'll move it to the other side of the room in case he's tempted to drink it. You have to think about bladders when you're chief carer. Only carer. It used to be my mother but she died. Died? Murdered more like.

It was her hip that did it. She'd finally got a new one. The unfortunate thing was if it hadn't been for her new hip, she would have probably been alive today, because that was why she'd gone out for a stroll, being able to walk properly after all those years and enjoying every minute of it. 'A teenager,' she said, 'I feel like a teenager again.' And I must admit it took years off her. It was a drunk-driver. Drunk? Kailoid if you ask me, not that I was there but there were witnesses. Mounted the pavement and sent her spinning about fifteen feet in the air. Quite gymnastic, really, considering a few weeks before she could hardly walk. Killed her outright, of course. I wouldn't have minded so much if he was sorry but all he got was a fine and banned from driving for a year. I know, I was there in court. Well, I mean, I know you can't bring them back, when they're dead they're dead, but who had to give up her house and her job and move back home to look after her dad? Me, of course. Muggins.

Ten to five. Have I got everything? Keys, sandwiches, flask, rug, notebook and pencil, opera glasses, gun? Check.

It's a glorious evening. Autumnal. 'The smell of cordite hung in the air.' I love that sentence, that sentence springs to mind every bonfire night. Used to read it in all the adventure books when I was a kid. Loved adventure books: cowboys and Indians, gunslingers, outlaws, spies, war, anything with guns in it. My mother, of course, didn't approve, thought little girls shouldn't read such things, kept giving me books about ballet dancers.

Cordite. I have a very strong feeling that it all started for me
with *The Man from U.N.C.L.E.* I used to watch it, well
everybody did, all my friends. Some of them had a *Man from
U.N.C.L.E.* gun. It looked like a Luger but I'm not sure what
a Luger looks like. I only say it looked like a Luger because a
boy in my road said it did and boys know that sort of thing,
or at least they pretend to. Anyway, the point is I didn't
have one. I could have had one, I suppose, if I'd asked, but
the trouble is when you're playing games with girls and
boys, and you say you want to be Napoleon Solo or Illya
Kuryakin, the boys tend to get petty and say, 'You can't,
you're a girl,' and then fall over laughing in a silly fashion,
which used to annoy me because of course they were right.
So I preferred to pretend I wasn't really that interested in
The Man from U.N.C.L.E. and I used a stick.

It was a very good stick, sort of Luger-shaped. I stripped
the bark off and painted it black, looked very authentic, I
thought. Hardly ever got to fire it, though, because most of
the time the boys only let us run around, scream a lot, get
captured and then get rescued again. So I was never able to
be the hero or even the starring baddie because, as the boys
said, 'Girls can't be heroes or starring baddies because girls
don't do that,' and of course they were right, girls didn't. I
saw it on the television. All the girls on the television ever
did was run around, scream a lot, get captured by the
starring baddie and then get rescued by the hero. So when I
found the gun I kept it hidden in my toy box, because I
thought if the boys knew I'd found a gun they'd take it off
me, because boys are like that. I carried on using my stick
because it wasn't a Luger-shaped *Man from U.N.C.L.E.* gun,
it was a real gun and it was heavy.

I fully intended telling my mother, but on the way home
with the gun tucked in my knickers – because I didn't have a
pocket in my dress – I started thinking what would happen
when I did tell her. She'd probably whip me down to the
police station and policemen frightened me. I thought they
might lock me up when I told them I found it on the
bombsite where we'd been specifically warned not to play.
Plus the fact that I'd hidden it in my knickers on the way

home. I don't know why I thought that was criminal at the time, but I did.

So I kept it hidden, only played with it secretly, on my own in my bedroom, a chair propped against the doorknob just in case. Oh, yes, I'd seen all the films, all the detective series, I knew what I was doing. I also heard about people cleaning their guns, so I polished mine with my mother's duster, polished my stick at the same time since I was still using it (well, publicly anyway). Then I saw a film with a man really cleaning his gun so I watched and copied – mine had bullets, I discovered. I played lots of games with my gun, secretly, on my own. I was, of course, always the hero, except when I was the starring baddie, because there was nobody there to tell me I couldn't be.

As it turned out it was very advantageous playing with my gun rather than reading books about ballet dancers because by the time I did come to use it I knew how to hold it and point it so that I looked fairly professional. Stupidly I did make the mistake of saying 'bang' as I fired it, habit of course, but I don't suppose he heard, or cared.

I was living on my own by then, had a fairly decent job, on the up and up as they say, so I got a mortgage on a little house. The area was a bit run down, a few unsavoury types, but I kept myself to myself. Mind you, I tried to be pleasant, said 'Good morning' and so forth, to the women mainly, I don't like to encourage the men, even if they are neighbours – well, you never know, these strange men you hear about, they've got to be somebody's neighbours, haven't they?

Funnily enough I'd more or less forgotten about the gun. I came across it when I was sorting out my bedroom ready for moving. I didn't know what to do. I couldn't just throw it away, I mean what if a child found it? I'd never forgive myself. It's not a toy, it's a lethal weapon in the wrong hands. So I thought, 'Oh well' and popped it into my suitcase and took it to my new home.

Actually, I don't know whether it was because I was living alone and wasn't used to it, but for a couple of weeks after moving in I started playing with it again. I suppose it's a bit stupid for a grown woman to be running around a house, sidling up doorways and shouting 'bang' to an empty room, but I couldn't help thinking it looked rather good as I caught a glimpse of myself in the wardrobe mirror, a gun held nonchalantly up, with my elbow resting on my palm, blowing imaginary smoke out of the muzzle. Well, it looked just as good as anything I've seen on the television anyway. It looks somehow more interesting when a woman does it, I think.

I was upstairs running my bath at the time. He was a noisy devil. I always thought they trained themselves to be cat-like. They always did on television, well, most of the time. They occasionally made the burglar noisy but I always got annoyed at that, thought, 'No, that's not right, that's a silly plot, everybody knows burglars are cat-like.' Well, mine wasn't. I turned the tap off and to tell you the truth I was shaking, and my heart, well, I thought they must be hearing it at the end of the street it was beating that hard. I heard him rustling about in the living room and I thought about the gun. I thought, 'If I lock myself in the bathroom with the gun I'll be all right.' I could have just locked myself in the bathroom, I suppose, but what if he kicked the door down? What if he wasn't just a burglar? What if he was a psychopath? Well, you hear such stories, don't you? No, I had to get the gun. It was in my underwear drawer in the bedroom. I mean, it wasn't particularly hidden, I just put it there because I didn't know where else to put it really, I haven't got a gun drawer and I'm too old for a toy box. And what if he comes upstairs and finds it? He might shoot me. He might take it away and shoot someone else. I'd never forgive myself if some innocent bystander got shot with my gun. No, I had to get it. He was still rummaging in the living room so I thought even if he hears me running from the bathroom to the bedroom I'll still be able to get there before he gets upstairs – unless he's particularly athletic, which is doubtful, because if he were athletic he'd know how to be cat-like. So I did it. I took a deep breath, told myself to be brave and ran. Well, needless to say he heard me, I'm no burglar, nothing cat-like about me.

But why he came upstairs I'll never know – I mean, why?

He obviously heard me, so he was obviously after me, so he obviously was not just a burglar. I think I was secretly hoping that he'd hear me and scarper the way proper burglars are supposed to. As it turned out we met each other on the upstairs landing. I didn't know what to do and I certainly couldn't think of anything to say, so I pointed my gun at him. I think he was a bit surprised because he backed off a few steps . . . I'd only wanted to point it at him, frighten him away. But when he looked at it, then looked at me and gave that funny sort of smile, I thought he was going to say, 'Girls don't do that,' and I thought if he does say that, I might not be able to and if I can't, he might. So I shot him before he said 'Don't'.

I'm not sure what happened next. There was a loud bang, and he sort of turned and stumbled, then fell down the stairs. My hand and arm hurt on account of shooting up into the air when I pulled the trigger, kickback I think they call it, very strange, made me go all tingly, I'd not pulled the trigger before. My head felt funny, but I think that's because my ears had popped with the noise. Anyway, I yawned a couple of times to try to get them back to normal as I went to have a look at him from the top of the stairs – he looked a funny little bundle lying at the bottom. I'd not seen a dead body before and I was quite fascinated, till he sat up and scarpered towards the kitchen. That was the most terrifying thing of the whole evening and I'm ashamed to say I nearly screamed out loud. I thought I'd killed him, made my heart turn over when he sat up.

I couldn't move for a few minutes, rooted to the spot I was. I felt worse, somehow, when he'd gone and it was all over. I knew he'd gone because the house felt silent again, the way it does when you're alone. Even so, I tried to move so that I could go down and check, just in case. Then I heard a loud bang outside – well, I nearly jumped out of my skin. I thought, 'My goodness, I've started a trend' – then I realised it was a firework. Bonfire night! Of course! Do you know, I laughed. I laughed and laughed, then I started crying, can't imagine why.

I moved house not long after that. Well, it's not the same

when somebody invades your privacy, is it? Took the gun
with me, of course, in my underwear drawer as usual. Mind
you, it was a good few years before I had to use it again,
only the next time I remembered the kickback. Nobody can
say I'm not a quick learner.

Living with my dad wasn't too bad at first, it made me
feel closer to him. It soon started getting tedious, though,
being saddled with the same old routine day in day out. No
intelligent conversation either – it's hopeless trying to talk to
him, he's too far gone.

I was going to get married, you see. I never thought I
would get married, I was always too plain and never very
good with men. Then I met Eric, at work. I'd never really
thought of Eric as a man, if you see what I mean, he was
always too fussy, too pernickety; in fact, at first I thought he
must be gay – nothing wrong with that, that sort of thing's
never bothered me, live and let live, that's my motto – but I
certainly didn't think I'd end up getting engaged to him.

When my mother died I was naturally very upset, and
since I'd come to rely on Eric more and more as I got to
know him, I was a bit disappointed when I didn't seem to be
getting the support I felt I needed from him. In fact, when
my mother died things seemed to get very cool between us.

At first I thought it must be me, because grief can do
funny things to a person and I know that Eric hadn't taken
to my parents in the way I'd hoped he would. But when I
mentioned that after we'd married Dad would naturally
have to move in with us, things got decidedly frosty. So I
suppose I wasn't that surprised when talk of wedding plans
stopped. I didn't mind that much, really, I had enough on
my plate with my father. I would have liked to have had
children, though.

The thing is it prayed on my mind. For months and
months I thought about that drunk-driver, and his paltry
fine and getting banned for a year. He should have been
locked up. I mean, people aren't safe on the streets while
men like him are allowed to drive around willy-nilly, getting
drunk whenever they feel like it and killing poor defenceless
old women with no comeback from the courts at all. She

was so happy with her new hip. The fine meant nothing to him, I could tell that. I went round to have a look where he lived – they gave his address out in court. I mean, he wasn't short of a bob or two: big detached house, not exactly scraping a living together. And being banned didn't seem to bother him, just got his wife to drive him to and from the station – I was there. I watched, I saw them – well, I had to get out and do something occasionally. Dad was testing my patience too far sometimes, no conversation, you see. Well, none to speak of.

I hated that man. I've always tried to get on with people, see the good side of them, but really I hated that man. He'd taken everything from me: my mother, my independence, my own home, my job, my future husband, my future children, well, my future life; in fact, my whole life. I was the one who felt locked up. I was the one who felt punished, and there he was breezing along as usual, off in the morning and back in the evening with his poor wife having to drop everything to chauffeur him everywhere. I felt sorry for her, I did, as if she didn't have enough to do looking after that big house and those little kiddies. She had to bundle them all into the car, drive him to the station, drop him off, drive back and bundle them all back into the house again. I watched them, when I could get out, when I had a few hours to spare. I sat on a bench in the park opposite. You had to crane your neck a bit, but you could see.

It was a good couple of years before I did something about it. I mean, it wasn't till 5 November that I actually got the idea, and then I had to wait a whole year. It was a funny year, that first year, having the idea and then having to wait. Sometimes I changed my mind and thought, 'No, leave it, you can't go around doing that sort of thing.' But when I decided not to I got depressed, started getting impatient with my dad, started blaming him for my predicament. I mean, it wasn't fair, was it, wasn't his fault he was ill, he didn't ask to have multiple sclerosis, wasn't him who killed my mother. It was that man, that drunk-driver, something should be done about him. Then I'd decide to do it all over again. And do you know, I felt happy? I felt my life had a meaning and a purpose. Everybody should have a hobby.

As it turned out I didn't kill him that first year. I didn't kill
him at all. I was going to. I went along, took my gun,
checked out the house, looked through the living-room
window. Nice house, but didn't think much to the furniture,
all modern, not my taste at all. Sneaked round the back and
saw the wife and children in the garden with the bonfire and
fireworks, then hid in the shrubbery in the front garden till
his car drew up – he was driving again by then – one less
job for his poor, hard-working wife. Then I was going to
step out and shoot him, but I caught a glimpse of his face as
he got out of his car. It was about half past eight, so it
wouldn't have surprised me if he'd stopped for a drink or
two on his way home from work. And then it flashed: I
thought, 'No, shooting's too good for you, one second and it
would all be over. And there's your poor wife, how's she
going to manage? Struggling to bring up those children
single-handed, and having to arrange for the disposal of
your body and belongings, and then not having a decent
wage coming in, probably, because she doesn't have time to
work because she's tied to the home and her dependants, so
all her friends will drift away because she can't socialise and
everything she wants to do will have to take second place
because everybody else's needs are more pressing and
there's nobody to support her and there's nobody to help
her and occasionally she might get a few hours to spare, to
do what she wants to do, but she feels so tired and unkempt,
and she's let herself go to such an extent that all she can do
is stroll around streets and look into other people's houses
and see what sort of happy and carefree lives they're living,
and wonder how it got to be that her life isn't worth living
because nobody bothers to ask her what she wants or what
she needs or how she feels because nobody notices her at
all.' No, shooting's too good for him. So I waited till next
year, came back, shot his wife. Remembered the kickback,
kept my hands steady and my arms straight. I'd like to see
how much time he finds to go drinking and driving and
killing old ladies with new hips now.

I've only got two bullets left. I used up the other two quite
frivolously, really. Silly of me, but I don't often get out and
enjoy myself. I'd become depressed. I didn't see anybody,
didn't meet anybody, I was just stuck in the house with my
dad all the time – a full-time job, multiple sclerosis, for both
of us. It got so bad I even started thinking about shooting
him and myself. Made a fool of myself in the doctor's one
evening instead. It was just after 5 November and I was
particularly depressed after having sat in the living room
listening to all the bangs and shrieks outside, and been
unable to contribute my own bang and shriek. I didn't tell
the doctor that, though. I just broke down in his surgery,
told him how cheated I felt and wept buckets. He was
marvellous, actually, did me a power of good. Gave me a
little pep talk about how I should pull myself together, look
on the bright side and not go thinking about what might
have been – or some such thing, words to that effect
anyway. Told me that family life wasn't all it was cracked up
to be, that having children wasn't just a financial burden but
an emotional one. And that women nowadays can do
anything and everything, even later in life when Father has
finally passed on. Do you know I came out of that surgery
beaming inside. I felt that good, that motivated, I
immediately went home and started planning. I shot his son
the next year, got him at one of those public bonfire dos. It
was easy to get him away from the crowd. I just told him his
father wanted him. People trust women. One less financial
and emotional burden for the good doctor I believe.

The last man I shot was a surprise on the way home from
the doctor's son. I shouldn't have done it, really, but what
the hell, I needed cheering up and besides, he was asking for
it, walking behind me in the dark, on a deserted street –
well, you never know, you hear such stories, don't you?

I saw Eric one year, my ex-fiancé, shopping in the high
street with his wife. They didn't see me. They were pushing
a buggy. I'm not keen on buggies, prefer prams myself, not
so common somehow. Eric's wife, Betty, used to be in my
class at school. She came from the local children's home,
didn't have parents, only a brother she was close to. I expect

that was the reason Eric married her, no in-laws to have to deal with, no sudden deaths of mothers or invalid fathers moving in. I don't think Eric can handle other people's grief. I'm not sure, though – see how their marriage holds up when I shoot her brother.

Talking of which, better get on, he'll be coming home from work soon and I might want to help him clock off.

Arsehammers

Beans on toast. It's always beans on toast when Grandad goes missing. I don't mind too much, it's just that Mom always clatters the spoon noisily on the plate when she's serving out the beans and she Talks! Like! This! About! Every! Thing! If she bothers to talk at all. It's at times like this that I'm glad Claudia's here. I don't like Claudia, of course, she's my little sister, but at least I can pick a fight with her and get Mom really shouting about something instead of Talking! Like! This! All! The! Time! And if Claudia and I get Mom shouting now, she doesn't shout so much at Dad when he comes home.

Grandad has been living with Mom and Dad and Claudia and me for years. Sometimes it seems like for ever but I can remember him coming. I was a lot younger then and remember that I couldn't make up my mind whether to be happy or sad. I was sad when Mom told me that Grandma had gone to live with the angels but I was also happy that Grandad was coming to live with us. I had pestered Mom for ages about Grandma changing her mind about the angels and coming with Grandad to live with us instead. I had, at the time, thought Mom would be pleased that I liked Grandma so much and couldn't understand why she got so upset when I asked. In the end I just wrote to the angels thanking them for having Grandma and asking that they take good care of her. Now that I'm older, of course, I feel really stupid about believing all that rubbish about angels, there's no such things as angels. Grandma is dead, buried and living alone.

And Grandad is living in our house. Well, so far. Because I've overheard Mom and Dad talking about being unable to cope and putting Grandad in a home. This worries me, because I like Grandad, Grandad's fun, Grandad's a hero to me and my friends, and Grandad's already living in a home, our home. But I'm older and wiser now and know that if I don't quite understand something it's always best to pretend I do and then get Claudia to ask the questions.

Having Arsehammers is magic. Sometimes you don't

have them and then, all of a sudden, bang, you have them
again. This is how it is with Grandad. Sometimes Grandad
will go out of the house to visit his friends to talk about wars,
or queue at the post office to talk about queuing during wars
and, after a certain time, he will come back again. Unless
the Arsehammers strike. Then Grandad will go out of the
house and disappear for hours, ending up in the strangest of
places and always miles away from his friends or the post
office. I often hear Mom on the phone or on the doorstep
with the police demanding to be told exactly how Grandad
managed to get himself locked in the cold meat storage
facility of the supermarket or into the staff canteen of the
foreign mail section of the postal sorting office. Mom doesn't
know. The police don't know either. But I do. Grandad has
developed a special kind of bottom. Hammer-shaped. And
when he wiggles it in a certain direction he is magically
transported to weird and wonderful places. A bit like having
special *Star Trek* powers but without the Enterprise.
Grandad could be waiting for a bus one minute and the
next – kaboom! – he is watching traffic go by on the
motorway. This is what makes Grandad special and a bit of
a hero. Because me and my friends have tried having
Arsehammers and it's impossible. At a given signal,
'Arsehammers!' we close our eyes, stick our bottoms out,
lurch them to the left, lurch them to the right, lurch them to
the left again, give a little wiggle, bend our knees, squat as
hard as possible and spring up as high as we can. When we
open our eyes we should be transported to weird and
wonderful places. But we're not. We're still in exactly the
same spot. Except once when Robert transported himself
further down the road. Which proves we are on the right
track but need practice.

　　Arsehammers is a game to my friends but to me it is
serious. I don't want Grandad to go into a home. I thought
that if I could learn to be transported like Grandad maybe
Grandad and I could go places together. Then Mom and
Dad wouldn't worry about Grandad being out all hours on
his own. I often watch Grandad, looking for clues.
Sometimes Grandad will be sitting in an armchair staring

into space. Mom will say, 'Grandad's not with us today' and I'll look at him, sometimes with binoculars, wondering where he is, exactly, and how he got there. When Grandad is here I often ask if, next time he goes, he'll take me with him. But Grandad just looks at me strangely and changes the subject. I find it very frustrating, and sometimes get cross with Grandad and warn him that he'll end up in a home. Grandad simply says 'Yes'.

When Grandad doesn't have Arsehammers he is just plain Grandad, and plays games with Claudia and me, or tells us stories about when he was a hero in the war. I like him then as well. There was a time when Grandad babysat but he doesn't any more because Mom 'doesn't trust him'. This is a shame because Grandad let us mess about before bed much more than Mom or Dad do and he never minded the bathwater splashing everywhere when we played Dive-bombing Ducks.

I like Grandad, I'm glad Grandad lives with us.

But Mom and Dad have decided that Grandad has to go into a home. Grandad seems to be permanently missing. And he's started shouting, which Mom thinks 'could get out of hand'. Claudia and I have been eating beans on toast for weeks on end, and Mom and Dad have been arguing for weeks on end, so when Dad stays home from work and spends all day on the phone, I know Grandad is doomed.

I sit with Grandad and Claudia in the back of the car, trying to make up my mind whether to be happy or sad as we drive out to put Grandad into the home. I'm happy because it is a day off school and Mom has made sandwiches for the journey, which means it will be a bit of an adventure going miles out of town. But I am also sad that Grandad is leaving. Mom and Dad have said lots of times that we can visit him at the weekends, but it isn't the same. And even though Grandad and I haven't run around the house playing Germans and British for ages, I was still hoping that some day we might.

By the time we get to the home I have decided it is definitely a sad day. Mom has made egg sandwiches, which I hate, and cheese sandwiches, which I hate even more than egg, and Claudia has been sick down her dress. However, I feel a lot happier when we go inside Grandad's new home. A lady with squeaky shoes shows us round the big house. Lots of other Grandmas and Grandads live here. And Grandad's room is a lot bigger than his old one and it has a television and a button he can press if he wants 'Assistance'. The lady smiles a lot and seems nice, so I ask her if all the other Grandmas and Grandads have Arsehammers. She says, 'Yes, this is a special home with lots of experts who try to make things better for your grandad and all the others like him.'

I am over the moon. It suddenly all makes sense to me. Grandad isn't being put in a home. Grandad is going to help save the world! Grandad is even more of a hero than he was before. Experts. *Experts* are going to train Grandad and all the other people with Arsehammers to transport themselves to proper places, planned places, where they can suddenly turn up and overthrow dastardly villains and listen in to secret spy conversations, and generally go where no man has gone before, and suddenly appear and say 'Boo' and frighten the life out of the most hardened of criminals. I laugh, I am happy, I think Grandad will be happy here too.

Mom is upset, though. In the car going home she cries. Claudia and I pretend not to notice but she cries a lot. When she stops crying and is just snuffling Claudia asks her why Grandad isn't coming home with us. Mom is quiet for a minute or two before she turns round to explain to Claudia that Grandad has a disease of the brain, which makes him very poorly and confused, so that he forgets where he is, where he is going, who he is and who Mom and Dad and me and Claudia are, and that he has to stay in that special home because he will get worse and worse. And then Mom starts crying again. I sulk the rest of the way home.

I sulk during tea, I sulk till bedtime and then, when I go to bed, I sulk in bed as well. I finally fall asleep deeply, deeply unhappy that Grandad doesn't really have Arsehammers and can't really transport himself and just turn up – kaboom! – anywhere. Grandad isn't going to save the world with the other Grandads and Grandmas and

Experts. Grandad is just plain Grandad and he is old.
Sometimes, I decide, I just don't like my mom.

Later that night I am woken by a loud clatter and a
thump. I sit bolt upright. There, at the foot of my bed,
stands Grandad. While I watch with amazement, Grandad
stands tall and proud, clicks his heels together, salutes and
bellows triumphantly, '*Arsehammers!*' Then, with a smile and
a wink, Grandad disappears. I stop sulking.

The next morning Mom tells me that Grandad has died
peacefully in the night. She tells Claudia that Grandad has
gone to live with the angels.

Later that afternoon I tell Claudia that there are no such
things as angels and that Grandad has simply
arsehammered his way back to live with Grandma.

Allotments

Politics? I don't know anything about politics, never been particularly interested, strikes me there's something wrong with the lot of them. Jean never trusted Blair, even before he got in, she said he's got funny eyes and she's not usually wrong.

Allotments, though, that's my subject. Allotments and vegetables. It used to be flowers but we've all had to make sacrifices. Well, I say 'sacrifices', but I suppose you could call it progress. No, no, progress would be vegetables *and* flowers.

You see our street, nice little street, ordinary, not much traffic, big enough gardens, ex-council, mostly, although some didn't buy, but we get along. Community, I suppose you'd call it. Most of us are pensioners, lived there years . . . nothing special. Well, nothing special on the outside anyway, nothing grand or fancy. Just an ordinary street, on the outside.

But . . . Well, I suppose it started a few years ago now, when *she* was running the country. None of us liked her. Jean said she was like that dentist who took over when Mr Billings retired – the one who gave me those false teeth that wouldn't fit properly – and she's not wrong. We had to change dentist in the end. I was having to eat soup for weeks. Mind you, you can't do that nowadays, so it's lucky we changed when we did, otherwise I don't know what we'd have done, because I do like to chew. And I say none of us liked her but most of us bought our houses, and why not? As I said, we'd all been there for years.

Anyway, Jack Bellows at number forty-four lost his job, made redundant, and he wasn't the only one. Early retirement they called it, but at fifty-five we all called it criminal, especially since his wife had not long gone. You see, when she died he went to work, kept working, kept his mind off it, I suppose, gave him a purpose. But without his job . . . not that he liked it particularly, panel beating, but anyway, he took it badly. Would just sit and watch telly all day and get more and more . . . well, he wouldn't wash, or eat or . . . anything.

So. I like to cook. I've always liked to cook, and garden,
when I've had the time, which I have now. Jean likes to
cook too. So we cook together, when we're not gardening,
and we chat and have a laugh and . . . well, it's quite
romantic, really. I tried knitting, Jean showed me, because
I've always admired knitting, I think it's a very useful
pastime for the evenings. Jean was always knitting away
while we watched telly. I'd get more and more annoyed
with the programmes but Jean would just knit quicker.
Much more constructive, really, when you think about it,
because she never felt the need to write to *Points of View*. My
letter got on once, but I was a bit disappointed. It wasn't my
voice and it came out sounding all wrong. I didn't bother
writing again, just started turning the telly off when I got too
annoyed, which is when Jean started teaching me to knit. I
wasn't very good. I suppose it takes practice. Well, I know it
does because Jean says so and she's not wrong but . . . I've
got a loom now. Helen from number seventeen gave it to
me when she got a bigger one. She does pottery, she's got a
kiln and everything so . . . We managed to get it installed in
the spare room. Fits just nicely with enough room for Jean
to sit with her knitting. She's got a machine now – she says
it's much quicker – but she still likes to hand-knit on
occasions. We put the telly in the corner to begin with but
what with the programmes getting more and more tedious
and neither of us being able to hear too well when we
pushed our shuttles across, well, we don't bother with it
now. Gave it to the Webbs when the licence ran out. We
pop round from time to time, but really, there's very little
we want to watch.

Anyway, the point is we cooked for Jack. We decided one
day that well, he was getting ill not looking after himself
properly and it would be nice to cook for someone else for a
change, so . . . And, of course, we chatted. He needed
somebody to talk to, or at least somebody to talk to him. So
we just went round one day with a vegetable flan and some
jacket potatoes – all allotment grown. Very tasty. Turned
his telly off, did a bit of cleaning, fed him and chatted. He

wasn't very forthcoming to begin with because, well, as Jean said, he wouldn't be, would he, and she's not wrong. And I must say to Jean's credit she persisted a lot longer than I wanted to. I got a bit fed up with him, to be honest, but as Jean said, what sort of a state would I be in without her and that got me thinking, I can tell you. So we went round every day for a couple of months and eventually he came round. Well, I say 'came round'. He liked wood. He'd worked as a panel beater all his life but what he really liked doing was things with wood. He just turned up on the doorstep one afternoon. Jean and I were having a cup of tea and a flapjack while we were waiting for our oatmeal loaves to rise. We were going through a porridge oats phase at the time. And there he was, stood on the doorstep with two little footstools: one each, handmade, beautifully finished wooden footstools.

So Jean was showing her stool to Mary at twenty-six, whose husband Ted has the allotment next to mine, which is how we got friendly in the first place. And Mary said she wanted some shelves put up, so of course she asked Jack and Jack agreed. He was slowly but surely coming round and, of course, working with wood . . . well, every little bit helps. But he said – and I think this is something to do with our cooking and my growing – because he said he'd only agree to do it if he could be paid by a weekly selection of fruit and vegetables for six weeks from Ted's allotment. And then, of course, Jack brought the vegetables round to Jean and me to cook for him. Unfortunately there was nothing we wanted that was wood. However, Cathy and Joe next door wanted a cupboard making and we wanted our bedroom redecorating – so we cooked for Jack, Jack built a cupboard for Cathy and Joe, and Cathy and Joe did our bedroom in a lovely combination of grey and pink, which looked very classy and not a bit twee as I'd worried it might. Meanwhile Cathy and Joe got interested in the allotments because I was talking about it while they were on their tea break from the bedroom. They were remarking on how tasty the tomato, lettuce and cucumber sandwiches were. So they got one too and Ted was happy to give them hints and tips on growing and composting, while Joe creosoted Ted's shed.

And that's how everything sort of started.

Now, of the sixty houses in our street twenty-two are allotment holders which, if you pool that among sixty houses, isn't bad, but it still requires extra vegetable growth in the back gardens, which is where my flowers went. Everybody said I didn't need to and nobody's ever pressured anybody into doing anything they don't want to, but I decided I would grow vegetables that had a certain beauty to them and of course fruit trees can look glorious in spring and harvest. In fact, every garden in the street now boasts some space for fruit and vegetables, if not the whole garden. And Kevin at number seven has devoted himself to polytunnels and a big greenhouse for growing exotics like lemons and oranges. He wants to concentrate on West Indian produce, which is very exciting (if a little doomed in our climate). Carol and Sue at number two have agreed to the communal compost heap because they're not keen gardeners, although even they have tomatoes every year and they're thinking of getting a goat. Mrs Williams does herbs, spices and herbal remedies. She's known locally as Witchy Williams, an affectionate name that she started herself. She's very good and Eve hasn't suffered from migraines since; she spends a lot of her time with Jacinta making chutneys, and bottling and preserving anything that can be bottled or preserved. In fact, their motto is: If it doesn't move, bottle it! And Ted and Mary now have an allotment each, and this year they've turned their garden into a wheat field as an experiment!

So, in the street we've discovered we've got two plumbers, an electrician, a chippy, a brickie, a painter and decorator, three plasterers, several cooks, knitters and sewers, a potter, weaver, nurse, van driver, spot welder, two car mechanics, a teacher, childminder, lathe turner, hairdresser, roof repairer and double-glazing salesman – but we don't really bother with him. Jane makes furniture from the willow tree in her garden and keeps chickens. And Brian. Brian has some funny ideas. Brian has a compost toilet. He thinks we should all have one but Jean put her foot down: she says she likes

her creature comforts even though she's never tried it.
Although Brian did offer. He invited us all round one day –
we turned it into a scrabble evening, but I noticed that Jean
kept her legs crossed all evening and refused any offer of a
drink, but I tried it and I thought, 'Why not?' He wants to
turn one of the back gardens into a reed bed water-recycling
system but nobody's volunteered.

Brian talks about wind energy and solar panels, he talks
about getting off the grid. He got Dave interested in dousing
for alternative sources of water. And I must say to Dave's
credit everybody now knows exactly where their water pipes
are, but that's as far as it's gone. You see, the trouble with
Brian is he's young, he's not been in the street long and
doesn't really understand our ways. He was very excited to
begin with and was happy to see how we operated, but I
think he's since started trying to take over, which has
annoyed some of us. He says what we're doing is political,
anarchic even. Of course, he's wrong, we're just being
neighbourly, but I don't think he understands that. Well, the
young don't, do they? I don't think the young understand
anything, really. Like my great-nephew Martin. He couldn't
understand why I was chuckling to myself that day I drove
him and his friends to Newbury to join the road protesters.
Brian, though, he thinks we should organise, publicise the
community. He wants to have meetings and do things
'properly'. Jean thinks he should get a decent haircut and
shave his beard off, and I think she's not wrong. He's very
entertaining but I don't think he realises we're mostly
pensioners. We want a quiet life; we want to just potter
along and help each other where we can; we don't want to
get into politics and meetings; we're not interested in politics
and meetings. Mind you, I say that but Ted was telling me
the other day that the government is getting rid of
allotments and building houses instead. He said that's
happening at the very same time as the Americans are
trying to take over the world food markets with genetically
modified something or others. I didn't understand what he
was on about, but he said it was in all the papers. Well, I
don't really bother with newspapers. Jean has one for the

crossword and bits about the royals but I use it to mulch. I was quite surprised, though, at how heated Ted got; he's usually such a gentle man. So . . . Ted thinks that Brian might be right, that our community might be political and anarchic after all, and we might perhaps need a meeting. I don't know, but if they are going to get rid of allotments, well . . . Allotments. And Jean never trusted Blair, even before he got in, she said he's got funny eyes and she's not usually wrong.

The Year of the Monkey

A church. A wedding. My daughter's. I'm not really there, miles away, napping.

There are dark days. And sometimes the dark days turn into dark nights and you wake up in dark days again. And one thing leads to another, each blacker than before till you swear that the blindness is permanent. But somewhere inside you, you hope to find the light switch, even though nine-tenths of you is saying there isn't one, and nine out of ten people are saying you aren't blind anyway. So you struggle in vain and in dark days. And all around the noise from the neighbours is deafening, increasing the isolation. Blind and deaf, deaf and blind, how to communicate, how to be part of things when you're blind and deaf? You can't see and you can't hear but someone, somewhere, out of the goodness of his heart is building wheelchair ramps. But don't complain, or you might be seen as ungrateful, even though in not complaining you are struck dumb. Blind, deaf and dumb. The year of the monkey.

A wedding. Shuffling out into the bright sunlight, bells pealing. My daughter.
   A helix. A double helix like a DNA strand. Merging and twirling and completing each other. That's how I feel when I touch her. My son too. Jonathan and Sarah, Sarah and Jonathan. My children. Touching my children. They're grown now, gone. And the house is finished, so I nap. A quiet stroll down the country lanes of my mind, I like to call it, when I'm feeling pretentious. Mostly, however, I call it a nap, although actual sleep has nothing to do with it.
   It's the before sleep, pre-sleep. Wandering off, strolling. Escaping this world, this life of social graces and béchamel sauce, and the occasional flap of a wedding or anniversary.
   Funerals are different.
   I'm always wary at funerals. Practicality is my middle name, on the outside. But inside my mind's awash with thoughts of ghosts and reincarnation and . . . and

something, something spiritual, something other-worldly, something the scientists dismiss as mere chemical combination.

God? No. Not the religious God anyway. Not the anthropomorphic God. Not sermons and holy books and thou shalts and shalt nots. It's something other, something else, something to do with pre-sleep and strolling and double-helix children. Totally natural yet unnervingly profound. Funerals – if I concentrate, if nobody interrupts – funerals have the same atmosphere, the same potential.

But weddings. 'Aren't you proud, Rose? She looks beautiful!'

Beautiful, yes. And so she should. We went to five different shops. She must have tried on hundreds of dresses, my feet were killing me, trailing around, back and forth, and you know what? She finally decided on the one she saw first. Typical, isn't it? So difficult, trying to get it right.

I wasn't needed, though. Sarah has a mind of her own, a very independent young lady. I went because she asked. She asked because it's the done thing. I wanted to be needed, I think Sarah wanted to need me, but in the end I was just company, somebody to nod or frown when asked, 'What do you think?' My function to second-guess whether she expected a nod or a frown. Get it wrong and I'd become a burden, a hindrance. Get it right and the mother/daughter scenario's complete. I'm well practised in getting things right.

Photographs. Smile! Say cheese!

People always interrupt. I suppose I don't mind today.

Funerals, though, I get incensed when people interrupt at funerals.

A time and a place for everything, they say, all the time in the world to talk about nothing. 'Julia! How nice to see you.'

'Rose! How are you?'

'Fine. So glad you could make it.'

Hate this strain, find it such hard work. Heard it all before. Same people, same sentences, put on their party frocks, party faces and do their party pieces.

And they're doing it today for Sarah. Because Sarah's going when I don't really know her, when we've lived this superficial relationship and ignored the churning undercurrents, disregarded the bubbling emotions, because it's not done to talk about them. Because now's not the time, now's never the time. All the time in the world to talk about nothing.

Have to content ourselves with clumsy hugs and quick pecks on cheeks.

'She looks beautiful.'

'A lovely do.'

'Marvellous day for it.'

'Beautiful, lovely, marvellous. Blah, blah, blah.'

Oh, shut up, you stupid people! Did the power of speech evolve for this? To be controlled, to be gagged by etiquette, manners? The middle classes invented as guardians of social conventions? Ensuring that nobody aspires to anything greater than knowing how to behave in public? 'How very kind.'

I watch TV but I hate it, it's so unrealistic. Every programme is dramatic, something happening, people in the middle of some big crisis. Life's not like that. Even the documentaries, which are supposed to be true, they're all about trauma, conflict, always somebody in tears. Nothing ever happens, or rarely. Tom and I, we've worked to be secure, strived to avoid all drama, tragedy as much as possible. The occasional death in the family, naturally, but even that's been expected. Of course I don't want tragedy, hate the pain of conflict – everybody does – but . . .

'Why don't you have an Irish wedding, Sarah?'

'Because we're not Irish, mother.'

'Oh, I'm sure there's a bit of Irish in us somewhere, there's a bit of Irish in everybody.'

We could whirl and twirl and drink and yeehaa! . . . We could get dizzy . . . We could get drunk . . . We could get sentimental . . . When Irish eyes are smiling . . .

'Oh, me poor wee darlin'.'

Touralouraloura . . .
'Oh, mammy I'm gonna miss you.'
Oh, Danny boy . . .
'And isn't your poor daddy weeping buckets over you,
even though you'll be moving in next door?'
I'm dancing! I'm flying!
No. Enjoyment is for people who don't deserve success.
'It's not done.'
'We're English.'
We don't have the emotional licence.
'It's noisy.'
'Crowded.'
'Drunken.'
'Messy.'
Too much like fun.

Sarah's a social climber, a career girl. I don't understand
her. She wears shoulder pads and bright-red lipstick, and
might – '*might*' – have children in her mid-thirties, possibly,
if everything's '*on track*'. There are no creases in her clothes
and I've got a sneaking suspicion this wedding is a career
move.

I've done it, I made it happen. A homemaker, housewife,
mother, drumming good table manners, please and thank
you, and never let the neighbours know your business. And
if you're taken for granted it's because your efforts were
seamless.

God, I want some passion, some drama.

I want Steven to have jilted her at the altar. She'd have
crumbled, the crowd would have muttered, gossip, tittle-
tattle, Sarah would have folded into her dress, creased and
weeping, and I'd have been there. Tom would've twitched,
paced, backed off, unable to take control, unable to fix it
and I'd have been there, flying in, reliable, sympathising,
comforting, the one she needed, the one she's always
needed.

Touralouraloura . . . Nothing to celebrate. Mothers are
never allowed to take part in celebrations. Pretend to be
important, look good, stay in the background or the kitchen.

Drama, though, crisis. Step forward two paces and take control. We've strived to avoid it, Tom and I. But what if Jonathan had been a drug addict?

And then there's Tom. The relationship with him, not knowing what it means, not quite able to grasp the undercurrents so easily.

Tom saying, 'God I felt so proud, leading her down the aisle. She looks beautiful, doesn't she?' Beautiful, lovely, marvellous. Tom. More like genetic engineering, a man-made double helix, half natural, half built. Maybe even two separate ones, which just happen to turn at the same rhythm. A strange emotional complexity.

Tom. Hanging on, on the outside, the periphery, the way men do. Wanting to enter, trying to enter, but somehow not quite making it, sometimes giving up, retreating, sometimes trying even harder.

'Come on, people, smile!'

The church. I like churches. Go into the church while it's empty, before the next wedding.

Cool, echoing, forbidding. They're supposed to be welcoming, these lonely places.

The vicar saying, 'Can I help you, madam?'

'Just wanted a quiet word with the Lord, vicar.'

'Oh, of course, of course.'

Idiot. Wouldn't talk to God, what's God going to do? It's like talking to a counsellor. They just sit benignly while you burble on, a half-smile or look of concern, or pass the man-size tissues, delete where applicable. They don't do anything. In the end you solve your own problems, usually by swallowing hard and learning to live with it. I can't even remember now why Tom and I went. Mid-life crisis, I expect. No, it was more than that.

It started years before. I couldn't explain. Can't explain feelings to people who don't feel them. It was after Jonathan was born . . .

Empty, aloof, I keep feeding him food but it isn't enough. I play with him, watch him, nurture him, bathe him but I don't know how to take him into this feeling. It's almost sensual but deeper. A natural, right feeling that's locked away in my inadequacy to express it. Start resenting the feeling because I can't use it, can't get it out of me, everything else goes grey.

Mother's death was the exact opposite but exactly the same.

The connection. I never realised it till then. In all those years we never touched that deeply. And her death made it too late. Must be some way of being on time.

I'm everything I'm not. I'm everything I could have been. I lie in bed and lead myself up the garden path. But not just in bed. Not any more. Just bed's easiest, no having to excuse myself, explain myself, beg anybody's pardon or hope to bluff. Bed's easiest, bed's where it started. Concentration's difficult, that's the point. I have to struggle to concentrate because really I'd rather be napping.

And then back outside, back to the sunshine and my father. 'I'm sorry, Dad, were you waiting?'

'It's all right, Rose, I'm in no hurry. And Jonathan's kept me company. I like to sit, pause occasionally.'

Pause? Nap. Feel it.

And then he says, 'I was thinking about your mother, Rose. It's a pity she missed it.'

Jonathan says, 'She was here, Grandad, in all our thoughts. Didn't you feel her?'

She was here, Jonathan felt her, Jonathan was napping.

And the reception.

What an expense, what a waste. Doing this because everybody else does it. And if we didn't do it? If Sarah didn't think it was important? If Sarah didn't think it was guaranteed to make the day special, make you enjoy it, the happiest day of your life, and then feel oh, so guilty because it's not? We don't know how to enjoy ourselves any more. Follow rules, told how it's done, how it should be done. The only thing wrong is that everybody feels the same but is afraid of saying.

And God, we're so comfortable, aren't we, all of us. It's
what we worked for, the ground plan that was laid . . .
when? Probably by our parents. Striving to be so
comfortable, to have no worries, no adversity, then putting
on party frocks and muttering banal epithets because our
lives are so lacking in . . . depth.

'Beatrice, Jack? I do hope you're enjoying the do?'

'Oh, absolutely, you and Tom have worked wonders.'
Wonders. We should be soaring, flying, leaping this social
barbed wire of struggling to find words innocuous enough to
remain polite. Of friendly, meaningless chit-chat.

I go to funerals now. It's a hobby. I sit quietly at the back.
There's another man. I see him quite regularly, I think it's a
hobby with him too. We don't speak, just nod. Nobody
seems to mind.

The atmosphere, I can feel it. The dead aren't dead,
they're hovering, reading our emotions, feeling us.

When mother died. The helix broken. My connection to
her wrenched away, stamped underfoot in one swift
moment. And I never said. I never asked if she felt it too –
till the funeral.

Till the funeral when I felt her there, felt her hovering,
felt her trying to repair the helix, both of us desperately
trying to reconnect, pushing towards each other, struggling
to reunite, to feel that feeling again, that feeling that was
never properly celebrated. Never acknowledged fully, taken
for granted, ignored while lesser, trivial, meaningless
nothingness was pursued.

People don't interrupt at funerals.

'There were things we never said, mother.'

'Things we never needed to say.'

'Didn't we?'

'We knew them, really, both of us. Besides which, Rose, it
was the feelings that counted.'

'Yes, but did we each know what the other was feeling?'

'Underneath it all we did.'

Underneath it all. Underneath it all.

Underneath it all's not good enough. Underneath it all

lasts a lifetime and what's the point of spending your whole
life keeping your true feelings underneath it all?

'Oh, Rose you worry too much. Does a DNA strand ever
unravel and separate?'

Only when you're dead.

And who do we hate? Who do we fear? Ourselves. Hate
our emotions. Fear expressing our emotions. And hate and
fear those with nothing to lose. People who dress differently,
act differently, whose priorities are not comfortable, middle-
class, humdrum, wall-to-wall, centrally heated tedium.
People with spirit, people with things to fight for. To fight
against us, to fight back because we demand they join or
suffer our march for comfort. A comfort that stifles and
bores us but God forbid we should ever let it go. God forbid
we should do something more useful than arranging jumble
sales for the NSPCC.

I think it's me. I feel it at funerals. Sat at the back on my
own, the man in the other aisle. We always sit in adjacent
aisles. Fred, I call him, Fred the stranger. We never speak,
just nod, a half-smile suiting the occasion. It would spoil it if
we spoke, we both know. Funny how disappointed I feel
when he's not there.

The pit of the stomach, brimming with emotion,
uncontrolled, animal, sexual, wading in mud and feeling.
Deep, deep howling.

I couldn't take Tom, couldn't even tell Tom, tell him I'm
going for a walk, he hates walking too, so I'm safe he'll
never join me. Tom would say, 'What do you want to go to
other people's funerals for? You never even knew them.' He
doesn't understand. Because the atmosphere, Tom, the
atmosphere is reeling with emotion, collective loneliness
concentrating our minds in on ourselves.

We're all there, disparate human beings, different
characters, personalities, lives, and we're all feeling our
solitude, together, wordlessly, honestly and muttering
pleasantries is the hardest thing, muttering pleasantries is
unnecessary, because nothing needs to be said, it's all felt.
Underneath we're all dogs howling at the moon.

Fred the stranger howls, I know he does, it's why he's there.

And the speeches, Tom's speech. 'Unaccustomed as I am to making speeches. Or rather getting a word in edgeways when the wife's in the vicinity . . .' Ha ha ha.

Tom's successful. Tom feels successful, but he's woken every morning by an alarm clock, ordered by a little piece of plastic machinery to move himself. Most times he doesn't want to get up, most times he wants to roll over, forget about life, but the alarm clock's the boss, the alarm clock's in charge. Even if he ignored the alarm clock he'd feel guilty, feel he ought to obey.
   And they say man rules the earth.

'Fathers and daughters, it is said, have a special relationship . . .'

Either he's changed or I have, I don't know which. There's nothing wrong, nothing I can put my finger on. It seems to be a steady hum of daily routine. No point in leaving for that. No point in leaving because someone's kind, considerate, willing. Because I feel somehow disengaged. Because I prefer it when he's not there, because when he's there I think, 'Get out, go away, get out of my house.' I want something else, something more. Something more than this dull, throbbing sense of resentment about . . . what? The inability to connect? To howl together?
   I don't feel in step, still feel like a youngster, waiting to start, waiting for it all to make sense. And I see Tom getting old and I realise my time's been wasted, used up. Spent my life preparing for life, spent my life waiting for life.
   I don't think anything will change by throwing everything up in the air and starting again. It's the 'underneath it all', I want the underneath it all. I just want to feel it. Be there.

A speech. I want to make a speech. I want to be there.
   'Unaccustomed as I am to blowing my own trumpet and making my voice heard, I'd just like to say to hell with the notion of traditional weddings, to hell with the archaic

giving the daughter away from one man to the other, father
of the bride, walking down the aisle, big important honcho,
while mother wears a hat and weeps. I would like to make a
speech for a change. I would like to speak as the ever
vigilant one, who lived daily, constantly with the chaos and
battle of clashing desires. I was the one who struggled, often
for a full ten minutes, to put a pair of Clarks on a wriggling
one-year-old. I was the one who had to deal with the kicking
and screaming temper tantrum of a seven-year-old in the
middle of Marks and Spencer's over something as simple as
the word 'no' to a chocolate Santa. I was the one who had
to bear the brunt of a scowling fourteen-year-old loudly
declaring her undying hatred of me in a seaside café in
Bournemouth. I am the one who lives daily with deep
powerful affection for the memory of resented times. And I
don't want to be the one who sits silently, in stupid frock
and frightful hat, while my daughter experiences one of the
most important events of her life! I love her. I hope she'll be
happy and I think Steven is a wonderful man. I wish them
all the best. Thank you.'

Did I or didn't I?

Jonathan clinks my glass and says, 'To you, Mom, you've
worked wonders.' Wonders?

The wedding or the outburst? The wedding, he's talking
about the wedding. He's talking about weeks, not years.

It's happening again, can't control it. I want to stay, talk
to these people, concentrate, stay fixed, firm, can't. I want
something to happen. I want something that I know is
happening. I want Jonathan to be a drug addict, a known
drug addict. I want everybody on their toes, waiting for
something to go hideously wrong. Jonathan upending the
tables in some mad psychotic outburst, Sarah wailing, her
day thoroughly ruined. Tom, exasperated, embarrassed,
trying to control him, ending up fighting. Steven joining in
like the new dutiful son-in-law. Chairs strewn clumsily aside,
food flying, guests in chaos, their hats comically askew.
Marzipan icing smeared on their best suits, silk ties ruined
by hurled red wine, everybody shouting, 'Oh, my goodness!'

Practical women frenziedly collecting knives, bottles and glasses, in case things turn bloody. And amidst it all I hit you all, I smack you generously round the face for daring to say what you're supposed to say, what it's done to say. I look you squarely in the eyes and shout . . . 'Speak up! Tell me what you're feeling! Take that stupid hat off and blow your top!'

We'd have something to talk about then, be a part of each other's feelings.

I asked Sarah if she was enjoying her day and she said, 'Yes, of course.' Then she added, 'A bit sad too, in a way.'

And I hugged her and said, 'Double helix. Don't you just love that word?'

'That's two words, Mom.'

Exactly. My point entirely. Touralouraloura . . .

Designs for Living

Part One

Music.

Louise *and* **Terese** *getting ready for a party, singing along together to the music, getting dressed, occasional dance routines, synchronised to relevant bits of song – obviously long-standing, habitual friends.*

Louise's *clothes and make-up: straight.*

Terese's *clothes and hair: lesbian.*

Dialogue while dressing.

Louise   Should I look straight, or not too straight?

Terese   There'll be straights there.

Louise   You said that last time.

Terese   There *were* straights there.

Louise   I never found them.

Terese   Maybe you weren't looking hard enough. Besides, you enjoyed yourself, didn't you?

Louise   I can't hang with you all the time.

Terese   Why not? Am I no fun any more?

Louise   You'll never get a girlfriend if I'm glued to you.

Terese   I can get plenty of girlfriends. And don't call them girlfriends, call them 'sex goddesses'.

Louise   Everybody assumes I'm your 'sex goddess'.

Terese   Fine by me.

Louise   Don't start.

Terese   Who's starting?

Terese *and* **Louise** *dance, sing, dress.*

Terese   Anyway you'll enjoy Marie's. Marie knows all sorts – lesbian, gay, straight, couples, singles, black, white –

pot-pourri parties she calls them. You might even find yourself a boyfriend.

Louise   I can get plenty of boyfriends. And don't call them boyfriends, call them pains in the bum.

Terese   Oh, like that again, is it?

Louise   I might go celibate. I might go lesbian.

Terese   Lesbianism second choice to celibacy, is it?

Louise   Don't start.

Terese   Who's starting?

Louise *and* **Terese** *sing, dance, make up.*

Louise   Politically I ought to be, but emotionally it doesn't ... you know ...

Terese   Appeal?

Louise   Yeah.

Terese   Yeah, I know what you mean. I feel the same.

Louise   Huh?

Terese   Emotionally celibacy leaves me cold too.

Louise (*sarcastic*)   Ha ha. (*Pause.*) How do I look?

Terese   Very good. Very straight.

Louise   Too straight?

Terese   Straight enough for me to keep my mucky hands off.

Louise   Don't say that.

Terese   Tut. Lighten up, Lou Lou.

Louise *and* **Terese** *singing more half-heartedly, serious preening and checking in mirror – touchy subject.*

Terese (*brightly*)   Anyway, more importantly, how do I look?

Louise (*brightening also*)   Very good. Very dykey.

Terese   Sexy dykey?

Louise   Very sexy dykey.

Terese   Will you be able to keep your mucky hands off?

Louise   Don't start.

Terese   Who's starting?

Louise   With no straights, you might be my best bet – only bet.

Terese   There'll be straights. A pot-pourri party, I promise.

Louise (*sudden doubt*)   Do you think I should put on jeans?

Terese (*long-suffering*)   No, just put on a jacket.

Terese *yanks* **Louise** *off in an effort to hurry her as* **J.J.** *paces on, restless, trying to create energy.*

J.J.   I should start. Just get ready and go. Go as what? Pinocchio? Party. Dictionary definition one: an evening spent drinking copious amounts of alcohol in order to handle boring chit-chat with people you either don't know, don't like or feel total indifference for. (*Pause.*) Marie knows all sorts, so I can be the drunk-in-the-corner sort. There's always one and it's always me – so without me, what sort of party would it be? A good one – probably. (*Pace.*) Oh, lighten up, J.J., it's just a bloody party. Party. Dictionary definition two: the by-chance meeting of the love of your life, whom you're not really chasing and are being very casual about, who will make life absolutely perfect once you've both sobered up and got rid of all the boring people that you don't know, don't like and feel total indifference for. (*Sudden stop, serious.*) Marie mentioned Terri. Marie said Terri was going, with her friend Louise. *Loooooooeeeezze*. I've never met Louise. Heard about her, heard all about *Loooooooeeeezze*, I even know her shoe size, but . . . Terri never mentioned Marie's party, so . . . I'm going. (*Pacing again.*)

Why do we do that? Why do we have parties? All cramming ourselves into one person's house, pretending to be sociable with ninety per cent strangers and having a thoroughly desperate time just because the party-giver wants to prove how popular they are. Dictionary definition three: an impossible-to-find crap place, blaring crap music and crap people mouthing moronic meaninglessness above the noise but hey, look at me smiling, laughing, having fun, these are my kind of people, these are my friends, I'm normal too you know, I'm just like you, I love a good party, I love people, I love sweating and swearing and vomiting into toilets at the end of the night. Why, I simply don't feel I've been *anywhere* unless I pass out at the end of it. (*Starts pacing again, agitated, obviously* hates *parties.*) Party. My definition: I can lie and tease and waffle and drink, and make up rubbish and take the piss and fantasise and drink, and be confident, above it all and solo and solid, And spend some time with Terri. And pretend I'm a part of people. And of course drink, did I mention that? Unless of course there's drugs – then I can *really* sparkle. It's a game, it's a game, it's a game, just put on a jacket and play the game, it's a good game, it's a fun game, my rules, my game, fun game. (*Then stops, picks up a jacket, decisively.*) Surely I can love someone enough *not* to want to have sex with them? (*Pathetic, self-deprecating look, jacket over shoulder, goes.*)

Music change – louder. Light change, party.

Louise *and* **Terese** *dancing sometimes together, sometimes apart.* **J.J.** *enters, hogs the drinks tables, watching, mostly* **Terese**. *Eventually* **Louise** *notices* **J.J.**, *likes what she sees.*

Louise (*to herself – euphemistically*)   Nice jacket.

J.J. *doesn't notice. When* **J.J.** *appears to be looking,* **Louise** *waves slightly, come-on style, but* **J.J.** *turns away to refill drink.*

Louise (*happily determined*)   Nice jacket *and* a challenge. Good.

J.J. *resumes drinking (and watching* **Terese***).* **Louise** *continues dancing with a bit more spark and laughter, showing off, trying to get*

J.J.'s attention, the dancing 'girly' – tits and arse. **Terese** joins in, funny, tits and arse show-off dancing with **Louise**, which **J.J.** notices and which irritates, requiring more alcohol. **Louise**, assuming **J.J.**'s watching her, doesn't notice when **Terese**, behind her, notices **J.J.** and, after initial surprise and embarrassment, stops dancing and waves – an obviously matey/male gesture. **J.J.** waves back with a grinning smirk. **Louise**, mistaking it for a wave at her, waves sexily back. **J.J.** looks quizzical, **Terese** looks embarrassed. **Louise** then notices that **Terese** has stopped dancing.

Louise   Do you two know each other?

Terese (*awkward*)   Friend of mine. (*Then to cover embarrassment.*) Pot-pourri, I told you, all sorts.

Louise   But are you a liar?

Terese   Huh?

Louise   Are there any rose petals in this pot-pourri?

Terese   Huh?

Louise nods her head in **J.J.**'s direction.

Louise   Straights? Are there any straights?

Terese assumes **Louise** is referring to **J.J.** being butch.

Terese (*guiltily dimissive*)   Oh, Lou, lighten up.

Louise   I'm light – and don't call me 'Lou'. I hate male names.

Terese, half exasperated, half friendly, grabs **Louise** and dances with her, formal and funny, but definitely 'male' for **J.J.**'s benefit and, as far as **Louise** is concerned, dykey.

Louise   And I'm not lesbian.

Terese   I know.

Slowly the dance gets formal and more serious.

Louise   And not all men are pains in the bum.

Terese   I know.

Then just serious and almost romantic, close, intimate, then very close, stop dancing, just looking at each other, then music stops, still looking, very close, very serious, almost a kiss then **Louise** *breaks away, glances towards* **J.J.**

Louise   Hot in here, isn't it?

Terese   Very.

Louise   Are there any straights here at all, Terese, have you seen one?

Terese   There are straights. But maybe straight isn't what you want.

Louise (*more serious*)   Don't start.

Terese   Who's starting?

Louise *walks away towards and passing* **J.J.***, so as* **Terese** *watches* **Louise** *go, she's half looking in* **J.J.***'s direction.*

Terese (*to herself*)   But I think you'd like to.

J.J. (*moving to* **Terese***, smirking, laughing*)   So that's the lovely Louise.

Terese   Don't take the piss, J.J.

J.J.   Would I?

Terese   Yes.

J.J.   Is this why you didn't mention the party?

Terese   You hate parties. 'Everybody's so desperate to get laid, everybody's so desperate to fit in, to have fun, to be popular and happy.' You hate happy!

J.J. (*still laughing*)   So you didn't mention the party because you 'desperately' wanted to wriggle around like a fish on a hook?

Terese (*losing it*)   Yeah, okay? Yeah, I wanted to wriggle around like a fish. I wanted to shake my bootee. I wanted to be popular and happy and *girly* – I *enjoy* it, okay?

J.J. (*still smirking*)   Okay.

Terese *stomps off. Music starts up.* **Terese** *resumes dancing alone.* **Louise** *sidles up behind* **J.J.**

J.J. (*to herself*)   I enjoy it too. Love it, in fact. Would love it more if we could . . .

Louise (*brightly*)   Talking to yourself?

J.J. *looks sideways at* **Louise**.

Louise   First sign of madness, you know.

J.J. *just looks – not impressed.*

Louise   Second sign is . . .

J.J.   Answering, yeah, yeah.

Louise   Enjoying the party?

J.J.   Not particularly.

Louise   Not your cup of tea pot-pourri?

J.J.   Huh?

Louise   Not your kind of party?

J.J.   Not particularly.

Louise   There we are, then.

J.J.   Huh?

Louise   We have something in common.

J.J.   Uh-huh.

Louise   So why come? To the party?

J.J.   I'm the local burglar. Thought I'd nick the TV while everyone was sweating.

Louise   Oh, right. Want a hand?

J.J.   Not particularly.

Louise   You're not being very friendly, are you?

J.J.   No.

Louise   I wonder why that is?

J.J.   I wonder.

Slight pause.

Louise   So you're not going to tell me?

J.J.   Tell you what?

Louise   The reason for your unfriendliness?

J.J.   That would require a degree of friendliness, wouldn't it?

Louise   That's true. And I suppose after watching me dance with a certain . . . (*jerking her head towards* **Terese**) someone, you're not prepared to give it.

J.J.   It's not really in my interests, no.

Louise   So I'm stuck here now. I've got to walk away rejected and dejected.

J.J. (*slightly warmer*)   Am I supposed to feel sorry for you?

Louise   You're the one who rejected me.

J.J.   Did I? I didn't notice.

Louise   Oh, I think you noticed.

J.J.   So how come I'm not smiling?

J.J. *and* **Louise** *exchange sarky looks.* **J.J.** *can't help but (finally) smile.*

Louise (*sing-song*)   You're smiling.

J.J. (*mimicking sing-song*)   Doesn't mean you're winning.

Louise *smiles back, thinking she's 'in' but* **J.J.** *turns to see* **Terese**, *debates a second, then . . .*

J.J.   Okay, wait for a gap and then walk.

J.J. *dances/shuffles sideways in rhythm towards* **Terese**. *Then both watch* **Louise** *pick up and dance alone.*

J.J.   Your mate Louise, you said she was straight.

Terese   Yeah, what about it?

J.J.   You said she just fancies men.

Terese   Just fancies men, she says. But . . . half the time she hates them so . . .

J.J.   And she insists she's not lesbian?

Terese   Insists. Why?

J.J.   Why? Because . . . she's teasing you.

Terese   She's my best friend.

J.J. (*half laughs*)   So?

Terese   We've known each other years.

J.J.   So?

Terese   Well, why would she tease?

J.J.   You tell me.

Terese   I don't know, that's why I'm asking you.

J.J.   What do I know about women?

Terese   Oh, don't start.

J.J.   Okay, maybe she's teasing herself.

Terese   What's that mean?

J.J.   Maybe she wants to but isn't sure. Maybe she loves you but doesn't want to stop being friends.

Terese   We wouldn't stop being friends.

J.J.   Wouldn't you? Sex is a very destructive thing.

Terese   How would you know? You never have it.

J.J.   Yeah, and I'm still here and smiling. And you're just *thinking* about sex and you're as gloomy as hell so I rest my case.

Pause.

Terese (*playing frustrated*)   What am I going to do, J.J.?

J.J.   Nothing. Do nothing till she becomes so overcome with passion that she can fight it no longer and just strips you and fucks you – and then tell her you've got a headache.

Terese   Seriously.

J.J.   I was being serious.

Terese   Have you ever fancied a straight woman?

J.J. (*laughs*)   You'd be amazed at what I fancy.

Terese   What have you done about it?

J.J.   Just put up another shelf – I've got a marvellous collection of books.

Terese   Trouble is, I really love her.

J.J.   Yeah, but do you love her enough *not* to want to have sex with her?

Terese (*thinks about it*)   Nah, not that much.

Both laugh as **Terese** *moves away.*

J.J. (*to herself*)   There's a million dykes out there who would think you were sexy and funny, and would want to spend the rest of their lunchtime with you. There's one over here, in fact, one right here, so why are you mooning around about . . . ?

Louise   You're doing it again.

J.J. *jumps, turns, looks at* **Louise** *and sighs heavily. An attraction disguised as dislike.* **J.J.** *more playfully aggressive than seriously so.*

J.J.   Look, can I straighten something out here? Do you fancy Terri?

Louise (*looking around*)   Who's Terry?

J.J.   Terri. (*Nods towards* **Terese**'s *direction.*)

Louise   Oh, Terese. No, we're friends . . . girlfriends . . . er, you know, mates – platonic.

J.J.   Yeah, yeah, I get the picture.

Louise   I'm not lesbian.

J.J.   Uh-huh.

Louise   I'm not against gay people, though, don't get me wrong. I mean, because I said 'I'm not lesbian' so quickly like that, you know, doesn't mean . . . I mean, some of my best friends . . . Ugh . . . Terese is my best friend so . . . but then you know her? Terese?

J.J.   Yeah.

Louise   You're friends?

J.J.   Yeah.

Louise   So you know that she's . . . lesbian?

J.J.   Yeah.

Louise   And you?

J.J.   And me what?

Louise   You're . . . ?

J.J.   J.J.

Louise   J.J. Terese has never mentioned you.

J.J.   Really? I'm flattered.

Louise   Strange that she didn't.

J.J.   Why?

Louise   Why not? I mean, she's my . . .

J.J.   Best friend, yeah, you told me.

Louise   So?

J.J.   So?

Louise (*expecting an answer*)   So?

J.J.   So what?

Louise (*getting exasperated*)   Tut. You're not helping, are you?

J.J. (*falsely getting exasperated*)   Helping you with what?

Louise   Isn't it obvious?

J.J.   Not to me it's not.

Louise   Well, why do you think I'm talking to you?

J.J.   Because nobody else will?

Louise   Oh, thank you.

J.J.   You're welcome, not at all.

Louise   I am obviously asking if you're straight or not.

J.J.   Oh. Well, it wasn't obvious to me.

Louise   So?

J.J.   So?

Louise   So?

J.J.   We've done the 'sos', we've already done the 'sos', move on.

Louise   Are you or aren't you?

J.J.   Am I or aren't I what?

Louise   Gay or straight.

J.J.   Well, why do you want to know?

Louise   What?

J.J.   Why are you so desperate to know?

Louise (*sighs*)   I wish I hadn't started this conversation.

J.J.   So do I.

Louise   Look, why don't you just bloody answer?

J.J.   Answer what?

Louise   Gay or straight?

J.J.   How about neither?

Louise   How about helping?

J.J.   Helping what?

Louise   Helping me.

J.J.   Helping you categorise? Helping you box? Number? Label?

Louise   Just helping the conversation.

J.J.   Oh, well, why didn't you say? I'd be only too happy to oblige.

Louise   So?

J.J. *gives a look.*

Louise   So I'm straight.

J.J.   Good for you.

Louise   And you're . . . ?

J.J.   J.J. Pleased to meet you.

Louise *gives a look.*

J.J.   Okay, to even up the numbers, so that everybody is included and we have closure on the problem, and since you picked blue, I'll pick pink and everybody is happy, and we can all sing 'God Save the Queen' and go home, and call a halt to this sad and lonely state of affairs and . . .

Louise   Oh, for God's sake!

J.J.   Okay, I'm gay. Obviously. What do you think?

Louise   Thank you! Now I know!

J.J.   Good! Glad to be of service.

Louise   Although I must admit I'm surprised.

J.J.   Huh?

Louise   Well, you don't look . . .

J.J.   What?

Louise   It's no wonder you're so bloody unfriendly.

J.J.   Bloody unfriendly? Who's being bloody unfriendly?

Louise   You are. And you know full well you are.

J.J.   Well, maybe I have reason to be.

Louise   Yeah, well, this is a pot-pourri party you know, if you want the 'pot' you have to put up with the 'pourri'!

Louise *stomps off, but pauses out of* **J.J.** *'s eyeline to catch another look.*

J.J.   Huh? (*To herself.*) Weird, weird, weird.

Terese   Who is?

J.J.   Your mate Lou, seriously weird.

Terese   Don't call her 'Lou', she hates male names.

J.J.   Oh, for heaven's sake.

Terese   Anyway, what do you mean 'weird'?

J.J.   Well, first of all I thought she fancied me, then she just buggered off.

Terese   Fancied you? Louise? (*Laughs.*) No, you're wrong there, J.J.

J.J.   It's not beyond the bounds of possibility, you know, somebody's got to fancy me sooner or later.

Terese   True. But Louise? No.

J.J.   Well, then she's just weird full stop.

Terese   Because she doesn't fancy you? Hah. The only weird thing about Louise is that she's fancied me for years but she won't admit it yet.

J.J.   Yeah, well, I'll go back to disliking her, then.

Terese   Huh?

J.J.   She's weird!

All three dance alone, slow, winding down, thinking. **Terese** *occasionally glances at* **Louise**, **Louise** *occasionally glances at* **J.J.**, **J.J.** *occasionally glances at both.*

Louise   The thing with pot-pourri parties is that you don't know who's who . . . or should that be what's what? Who's what? Who does what to whom? Who wants to do what with whom? . . . Anyway, whatever, you know what I mean.

Terese   You fancy someone, then?

Louise   You promised me straights, Terese. You promised.

Terese   Ugh, don't start.

Louise   Who's starting?

Terese   What's so great about straights anyway? They're boring.

Louise   Thank you.

Terese   Not you, them.

Louise   Are you getting at me?

Terese   Why should I be getting at you?

Louise   Well, why not? You're the one with the hankering.

Terese   What?

Louise   Doesn't matter, forget it. So you think I'm boring, do you?

Terese   I never said that . . .

Louise   You did. You said straights were boring. Therefore you think I'm either boring or I'm really desperately dykey but I'm pretending not to be just to . . . what? Irritate you, I suppose?

Terese   Lighten up, Louise. What's eating you all of a sudden?

Louise   Well, how would you like it if I said you were boring? If I said you were just pretending to be lesbian because . . . because . . . I don't know . . . because you were frightened of male anatomy winking its one good eye or something.

Terese   Male anatomy winking its . . . ? (*Starts laughing.*)

Louise   And now you're laughing at me.

Terese   I'm not. I'm laughing at male anatomy.

Louise   Whatever. It's not funny, it's tedious.

Terese   Oh, come on, Lou . . .

Louise   Don't call me Lou.

Terese   Oh, come on, it's late, we're tired, we're drunk, we're not going to get laid. Lighten up. So what, who cares?

Louise   I care! I care. It's always the same with you. You say, 'Oh, come to this party, there's bound to be straights there', and there never are. 'Let's go to this bar or let's go to that club' – always gay . . .

Terese   That's not fair because you . . .

Louise   And I go along because we're friends. I don't complain, I don't say 'Oh, everybody's boring', I don't ask you to go to straight places . . .

Terese   I go to plenty of straight places.

Louise   Oh, really? Where?

Terese   The cinema.

Louise *gives a look.*

Terese   You never want to go anywhere else! You never want to go to straight places – straight clubs give you the hebes, you said so!

Louise   Doesn't give you the right to criticise my sexuality.

Terese   I am not criticising your sexuality.

Louise (*almost interrupting*)   How would you like it if I criticised your sexuality?

Terese   You can't criticise a dyke's sexuality, we look too scary.

Louise (*on a roll*)   Oh, you think so, do you? You don't think it's laughable that you dress like a boy and say you like girls? Dress like a boy and say you hate men? Say you're a woman and hide all your girly knee-jerk secrets from the rest of your dykey friends. Like Karen, wiping every trace of femininity and then daring you to call her manly, defying you to laugh at her Sisterhood of Satan motorbike club. You want to be invisibly sexless, with all your true feelings safely locked away behind a pair of baggy combat trousers and a sports bra. You know your trouble, Terese . . .

She notices **Terese***'s silent, staring reaction.*

Your trouble is I've said too much and now you're going to take it personally and this pot-pourri has lost all its fragrance.

Pause.

J.J.   Mind if I join you?

Louise   Yes.

Terese   No.

Louise *makes a face, then backs down, shrugs.*

Terese   Sit down, J.J., pull up a floor, nice to talk to a friendly face for a change.

J.J.   Don't know as I'd call it a friendly face but . . .

Louise   Finally, agreement.

J.J.   But people do seem to interrupt it a lot.

Louise   Especially when it's talking to itself.

J.J.   Finally a definition of 'two-faced' that makes sense.

Terese   Talking of 'two-faced', I'm assuming you've met Louise?

J.J.   We have locked horns already, yeah.

Louise   Humph.

J.J.   I'm not too sure what we were arguing about but . . .

Terese   Invisible sexlessness, possibly.

J.J.   Huh?

Louise   I didn't mean it like that and anyway you started it.

Terese   I did not.

Louise   You were criticising my sexuality.

Terese   I was not. I don't give a toss about your sexuality.

Louise   Oh, yes, you do.

Terese   Don't.

Louise   You'd love it if I was a lesbian.

Terese   Wouldn't.

Louise   Would.

Terese   Wouldn't.

J.J.   Would.

Terese   Mind your own business, J.J.

J.J.   Well, you would.

Terese   Yeah? So? Doesn't mean I love her any less because she's not!

J.J.   Oh, I think it does. I think it could, because it means having to put the brake on your personality and emotions, swallowing your instincts and keeping your true feelings safely locked . . .

Terese/Louise   Oh, shut up!

Silence for a while.

J.J.   So is this the dope corner or what?

Louise   No, this is the women's corner.

J.J.   Women's corner.

Louise   Lesbian corner.

Terese   Lesbian corner?

Louise   Where lesbians talk. We talk lesbian talk – very exclusive.

Terese   Lesbian talk?

J.J. (*shrugs*)   Similar to Polish perhaps.

Terese   What's lesbian talk, Louise?

Louise   It's stuff you talk as a prelude to this . . .

Louise *leans right across* **J.J.** *in order to kiss* **Terese**. **Terese**, *disarmed, falls backwards with* **Louise** *on top.* **J.J.** *uncomfortable, believing it to be a dig at her, that* **Louise** *somehow knows* **J.J.**'s *desire for both.* **Louise** *and* **Terese** *finally resume positions.*

Terese   Is that some sort of apology?

Louise   Some sort of apology.

J.J.   So nobody's got any dope, then?

Louise   'fraid not.

J.J.   Going to have to do this lesbian talk then, aren't I?

J.J. *leans over and kisses* **Terese**. **Terese** *surprised.*

Terese (*after*)   J.J.?

J.J.   I must have done *something* to be sorry about.

J.J. *and* **Louise** *stare challengingly at each other, both knowing what each really wants.*

Terese   What's going on here? Am I missing something?

Louise (*overdramatic*)   Terese, I'm so sorry . . .

Louise *kisses* **Terese** *again,* **Terese** *bemused but willing. Then* **Louise** *and* **J.J.** *challenging again.*

J.J.   Terri, can you ever forgive me?

J.J. *moves to kiss* **Terese** *again.*

Terese (*as* **J.J.** *approaches*)   Not again!

Then slight hesitation before, with passion, **J.J.** *and* **Louise** *kiss, to the confusion of* **Terese**.

Terese (*trying to get in*)   I'm sorry too, you know. I want to apologise too . . . (*Finally sighing.*) I've got a headache.

Louise *and* **J.J.** *separate.*

Louise   And I think it's time to go home. (*To* **J.J.**) Wait for me.

Louise *exits.* **Terese** *and* **J.J.** *very confused about what the 'Wait for me' implies.*

Terese   'Wait for me'? What does she mean, 'Wait for me'?

J.J. *shrugs defensively, worried.*

Terese   She wants you to wait for her. She wants to go home with you! You, you!

J.J.   Seemingly, yeah.

Terese   Well, thank you very much!

J.J.   What?

Terese   You've scored, with Louise, *my* Louise. The woman I'm crazy about, the woman I've lusted after for years. She even kissed me. That dream, that dream of finally something more than the occasional peck on the cheek, or 'how you doing' hug. It finally came, finally got it. Just when I thought she hated me . . . *just* when I started hating *her* . . . And then she turns round and goes home with you! Although God knows what she sees in you.

J.J. (*murmurs*)   More than there is, obviously.

Terese   What?

J.J. *shakes head dismissively.*

Terese   How can she reject me and then turn round and embrace you? I mean, you're more dykey, you're bigger than dykey, you're beyond a dyke! How could you, J.J.? I thought we were friends.

J.J.   It's not my fault.

Terese   Well, then, whose fault is it?

J.J.   I don't know, it just happened.

Terese   She can't possibly like you, she's straight and you're . . . you're . . .

J.J.   She can't come home with me. I don't want her to.

Terese   Well, you should have thought of that before you started stirring it.

J.J.   I wasn't stirring it. (*Slight pause.*) Look, you take her home with you.

Terese   Oh, and finish what you started, I suppose.

J.J. (*starts laughing*)   Yeah, good idea.

Terese   I'm not joking, J.J.!

J.J. (*defensively*)   It's funny.

Terese   It's not.

J.J. (*drops to serious*)   No, you're right, it's not.

Terese   What I really don't understand is what have you got that I haven't?

J.J.   Better jackets?

Terese   I said don't turn this into a joke, J.J.

J.J.   But it is a joke, Terri. (*Sighs, having to say it.*) She thinks I'm a bloke.

Terese   What?

J.J.   She thinks I'm a guy.

Terese   She doesn't?

J.J.   She does.

Terese (*laughs hysterically with relief*)   Oh, thank God for that.

J.J.   Excuse me?

Terese   Well, that's all right, then. Simple. You can just explain, just tell her you're not.

Louise *briskly entering.*

Louise   'Tell her you're not' what?

Terese   An optician.

Terese *laughing as* **J.J.** *ushers her to leave.*

J.J. (*jumping in*)   Er . . . not used to er . . . people like you.

Louise   Don't worry, I'll understand if afterwards you still prefer men . . .

Terese   What? Hang on a minute . . .

Terese *about-turns but* **J.J.** *forcibly moves* **Terese** *in the direction of off.*

Louise   And gay guys, well, they're different from straight guys, I imagine.

Terese   Er, Louise? I think J.J. needs to talk to you.

J.J.   Yes. Talk, yes.

Louise   I don't mind just talking if you're . . . nervous about it.

Terese   I think you should talk. Oh, boy, do I think you should talk. (*Laughing as definitely going.*)

Slight pause as **Louise** *and* **J.J.** *ensure* **Terese** *has gone.*

Louise   Is Terese mad with me?

J.J.   No she's just . . . mad.

Louise   I know it can be difficult because she does . . .

J.J.   Fancy you.

Louise   Yeah.

Louise *comes close to* **J.J.**, *touches.* **J.J.** *moves away, awkward.*

Louise   Not used to women, are you?

J.J.   Um . . . Look, Louise . . . it's . . . I got to be up for work in the morning and it's late and . . .

Louise   Where do you work?

J.J.   In a bar . . . um . . .

Slight pause.

Louise   I didn't have you down as someone who was gay. You don't look a bit gay. Still, that's every woman's fantasy, isn't it? To turn a gay guy straight with only the power of her thighs at her disposal. Well, not every woman's. Just mine, in fact. Right here, right now, this moment anyway. Tomorrow, who knows? I might make love to you all over again, or I might just kick you out of bed and tell you to go back where you belong. What do you think it's going to be?

J.J., *totally lost for words, caught dumbstruck and awkward, manages only a shake of the head.*

Louise   Totally presumptuous of me, though, isn't it? Saying you don't look a bit gay. As if gay looks a certain way – what did you say earlier? Something about categories? Boxes? You don't want to be boxed, do you, J.J.?

J.J. *still managing a shake of the head.*

Louise   You want to be vamped, don't you?

J.J. *moves away, dead quick.*

J.J.   No, I don't think so.

Louise   You've gone very shy. You were more confident at the party.

J.J.   It . . . er . . . depends on the situation.

Louise   And what control you have over it.

J.J.   Exactly.

Louise   And what control do you have?

J.J.   Louise . . . erm . . .

Louise   Are you losing it, J.J.?

J.J.   Oh, yes.

Louise   Shall I take control, then?

J.J.   No.

Louise   Take control of you?

J.J.   No, I don't . . . think . . . so

Louise *stands and starts undressing.* **J.J.** *really in two minds, turned on but panicking at the situation.* **Louise** *undresses as far as whatever, then approaches* **J.J.**, *pushes her to sitting, then sits on* **J.J.**'*s lap.*

Louise   So.

J.J. *stands up suddenly,* **Louise** *falls.*

J.J.   No . . . this is . . . I can't.

Louise   Weren't you turned on?

J.J.   This is . . . it won't . . . it's a mistake . . . you've got me wrong, Louise . . . erm . . . talk. Let's just talk.

Louise   You were turned on.

J.J.   Look. I really like you, Louise, but I really think we should . . . erm . . .

Louise   Weren't you. You were turned on, weren't you?

J.J.   Yes. Yes but . . .

Louise   Well, then.

Louise *approaches again.*

J.J.   No. No, Louise, you've made a mistake.

Louise   Have you had women before?

J.J.   That's not the point.

Louise   Have you? Or am I the first?

J.J.   It's not the point.

Louise   Okay, I'll imagine I'm the first.

Louise *grabs and kisses* **J.J.**

J.J.   Louise, Louise we can't go any further.

Louise   Shh, shh, let me take control.

While kissing again, **Louise** *manoeuvres* **J.J.** *back to seat/floor/wherever, so that* **J.J.** *is more or less pinned down.*

J.J.   Louise I'm not a gay . . .

Louise *covers* **J.J.** *'s mouth.*

Louise   And I'm not a moron.

J.J. *very surprised.* **Louise** *resumes kissing again and makes love as far as is possible with* **J.J.** *fully (or partially but covered) clothed.*

Part Two

Louise *bounces on, full of the joys.*

Louise (*singing*)   'I feel pretty, oh so pretty, I feel pretty and witty and gay.' Well, not gay exactly, that's not strictly true. (*Starts pacing.*) I should tell her. Just go round and tell her. Tell her what? Fantasy? Romance. Dictionary definition one: two eyes meet across a crowded sea of alcohol. Is J.J. male or female? I don't care, Terese. I've just had a vaginal romance and the vagina wasn't yours, I'm sorry. (*Pause.*) Terese is the lesbian, Terese is the sure one, I've never been that sure. I remember when she told me, came out to me, I envied her, it was exciting, it was like a statement of belief, a statement of intent. I was going to be a princess when I was three. I put a towel over my head and married the mirror when I was five, those are the only statements I've ever made. (*Pace.*) Oh, lighten up, Louise, it's just a bloody romance. It's never going to last. Romance. Dictionary definition two: the endless searching for Mr Right, who's always wrong. Or maybe I am. Or maybe my sneaking suspicion that life is just compromise and irritation is right and there's no such thing as satisfaction, perfect couples, happy ever after, or even, let's face it, a full-blown, blistering, soak-the-sheets orgasm. Well, not with the guys I've met anyway. But J.J. . . . J.J. Terese . . . and what do I do when Terese says 'But I could give you a full-blown, blistering, soak-the-sheets orgasm'? Do I say, 'Okay, you've got five minutes, do your worst.' That's not the point, Terese, you're my best friend, J.J. just turns me on. (*Sudden stop, serious.*) I've been to lots of gay places with Terese and the butch ones, the *really* butch ones, they've always fascinated me. There's always been a certain . . . attraction. Like Karen, I think I could have . . . got into Karen – beautiful, bike-riding brickie with a bum crack – if she'd had the courage of her convictions, if she'd admitted to being male, if she hadn't been so scary. I knew what J.J. was, of course, well, not straight away – if I'd known straight away I wouldn't have . . . played. It's only a game. A *good* game, but a game nevertheless. (*Pacing again.*) Why did I do that? Why did I go for J.J.? Because J.J.'s sexy, and messes about, and lies, and won't tell the truth, and won't be labelled. And J.J.'s the best guy I've met. (*Starts pacing again, agitated, obviously* hates *the thought of telling* **Terese**.) Romance. My definition: we can make love and tease and play and fantasise, and make up our lives and our roles and take the piss and fantasise and love, and be confident, above it all and together and solid. And spend some time with Terese and pretend, this time, I'm the interesting one. And pretend I'm a part of J.J. And of course fantasise, did I mention that? Unless, of course, this is for real – then I'm *really* confused. (*Then stops, decisive.*) Surely Terese can love me enough *not* to want to have sex with me? (*Look of comical doubt.*) Well, one way or the other I've got to say something – otherwise J.J. will.

Louise *off one way as* **J.J.** *comes on the other, hotly pursued by* **Terese**.

Terese   So?

J.J.   So?

Terese   So?

J.J.   Everybody keeps 'so-ing' me lately, it's getting very disconcerting.

Terese   So?

J.J.   You're doing it again!

Terese   Just tell me what happened.

J.J. (*shrugs*)   Er . . . nothing.

Terese   Nothing? Can't be nothing, something must have happened.

J.J.   Erm . . . not really.

Terese   Well, so, she thinks you're . . . ?

J.J.   Fabulous.

Terese (*sarcastic*)   Yeah, right. Come on.

J.J.   Come on what?

Terese   Oh God, J.J., you are exasperating sometimes! What were you playing at?

J.J.   I just said I was gay.

Terese   A gay bloke.

J.J.   I just said gay.

Terese   And she thought you were a gay bloke.

J.J.   Erm . . . no, not really.

Terese (*sighs heavily*)   J.J., what happened?

J.J.   I don't know. Nothing. She didn't come. She went home.

Terese *frowns, not convinced.*

J.J.   Okay, if you want the absolute truth . . . I ran away.

Terese   What?

J.J.   I ducked down a side road and then . . . just ran.

Terese   You did what? That's awful.

J.J.   I know but when you're in that situation – it was a great situation . . . sort of. I mean, somebody saw me as me. Somebody accepted and went along with and . . . But of course, what could I do? I can't follow through. Have you any idea how frightening it is when someone you like thinks you're . . . something else and . . . they're going to find out?

Terese   You left her on her own, in the middle of the night, on a dark street, in a strange place?

J.J.   Er, yeah.

Terese   With her looking . . . straight? . . . Feminine . . . Vulnerable?

J.J.   Don't push it, Terri, she's not a damsel in distress, you know. I mean, God what happened to feminist credentials?

Terese   She might not have had any money, she might not have been able to get a taxi, she might have been lost . . . she might . . .

J.J.   She'd have phoned you, wouldn't she?

Terese (*swiftly drops the concern*)   Oh, yeah, that's true. So, no big story, then?

J.J.   Nope.

Terese   You do realise that I don't believe a single word, don't you?

J.J.   All right, all right, we made mad passionate love all night, with her on top, making all the moves, and me, I was just putty in her hands – it was sensational, the earth moved, it was a night I've dreamt about since . . . oh, time immemorial.

Terese   So you talked.

J.J.   Yeah.

Terese   Did she still think you were a bloke?

J.J.   Yeah, no, I don't know, the question never arose.

Terese   I thought that was the question.

J.J.   Yeah . . . but . . .

Terese   You just didn't bring it up.

J.J.   No.

Terese   You just talked about . . .

J.J.   Generally. Just talked generally.

Terese   So . . . ?

Terese *shrugs as though no story,* **J.J.** *does the same.*

J.J.   Oh, yeah, and we had toast.

Slight pause.

Terese   So did she talk about me at all?

Pause. **J.J.**, *awkward, tries to talk seriously.*

J.J.   There's a million dykes, you know, Terri, millions. And you could get . . . at least one of them.

Terese   Sorry, is that a compliment?

J.J.   You know what I mean. You're a typical dyke.

Terese   Is *that* a compliment?

J.J.   I don't understand why you're spending all your time and energy . . . I mean, for what? I always thought it was the code, you know? 'Don't chase straights.' And you are so . . .

Terese   Typical?

J.J.   You have no problem fitting in. Nobody's going to think there's anything . . . odd about you, you know, when you're yourself, relaxed, whatever. So why . . . ?

Terese   She didn't mention me, did she?

J.J.   No.

Terese   Not once?

J.J.   Maybe once. Or twice.

Terese   What did she say?

J.J.   Oh, Terri.

Terese   What?

J.J.   I don't know.

Terese   Was it good or bad?

J.J.   I can't remember.

Terese   You must remember.

J.J.   Well, I can't.

Terese   You must remember whether somebody's saying good things or bad things about your friends?

J.J.   Well, I can't, okay?

Terese   So, you don't see me as a friend, then?

J.J. (*sighs*)   Look, Terri, I met somebody last night who saw me as . . . I don't know, male, female, gay, straight, whatever, I don't know but . . . it was good, it was great, it's what I love. It's meaningless – to other people. But to me . . . it doesn't happen often, but when it does . . . when it does I really don't get the urge to spend my time jotting down notes about what they might have said about you. Okay? Now I'm sorry, I think you're my friend, I hope you're my friend and as such, I would hate to do anything to hurt you but . . . what she might have said about you I don't know, I can't remember and I really don't care.

Terese   Nothing major, then?

J.J.   No, nothing major.

Slight pause.

Terese   I was really jealous of you last night.

J.J.   What?

Terese   The way you kissed Louise. There was something about you that was . . . you looked great.

J.J.   Me and Louise?

Terese   Yeah, but . . . mostly you. And what you just said about being male, female, whatever . . . I think I sort of saw it last night, so . . . and I just wanted to say, I don't think it's meaningless. In fact, I quite envy it.

J.J.   Envy what?

Terese   Louise mistaking you, your enjoyment of it.

J.J.   Mistaking me?

Terese   Mistaking you for what you're not.

J.J.   I don't enjoy being mistaken for what I'm not, Terri, I enjoy being taken for what I am.

Terese   Yeah, but . . . what are you?

J.J. (*shrugs*)   Something else. Something other, not male, not female, but something both. Female body, male essence – something. Salt and pepper in one pot. Great idea but not for everyone.

Terese   Perhaps it could be for everyone.

J.J.   Perhaps you're getting a bit serious.

Pause, looking at each other – realisation of mutual attraction.

Terese   Shall we . . . get back to taking the piss now?

J.J. (*with relief*)   Yeah, let's.

Terese (*with relief*)   That was close.

J.J.   Too close.

Terese   So this once or twice that she mentioned me, was it a big once or twice or was it just a passing once or twice?

J.J.   Ugh!

Terese   Well, just look what the cat dragged in.

Louise   It hasn't been that long.

Terese   You couldn't drop by? You couldn't phone? You couldn't write?

Louise   All right, all right, I'm sorry.

Terese   I could have been lying dead on the carpet.

Louise   Okay, I'm sorry.

Terese   Blood pouring, pulse diminishing.

Louise   All right!

Terese   So. Tell me.

Louise   I've been busy. Met someone.

Terese   Obviously. What's he like?

Louise   Erm . . . different.

Terese   Different how? Different he's got two dicks or different it might last this time?

Louise   Oh, I don't think it's going to last.

Terese   Going downhill before you've climbed the romantic heights, that's novel, that's different.

Louise   I don't really know how to tell you, it's sort of complicated.

Terese   He's married.

Louise   No.

Terese   He's in prison.

Louise   No. Although symbolically I suppose you could say.

Terese   He's not a poet, is he?

Louise   No.

Terese   Thank God for that. So what's his name and where did you meet?

Louise   Erm . . .

Terese   Oh, come on, it can't be difficult to tell me his name.

Louise   Well, yeah, it's difficult.

Terese   He's Russian.

Louise   We met at the party.

Terese   Which party?

Louise   The pot-pourri party.

Terese   Marie's?

Louise Yeah.

Terese But there weren't any straights there.

Louise I knew it! I knew there weren't. You're always telling me there's going to be and there never are.

Terese All right, don't start.

Louise Who's starting?

Terese Anyway, you left with J.J.

Louise Yes.

Terese And you talked all night.

Louise Sort of.

Terese Well, that's what J.J. said.

Louise And J.J. was right to say that, that's what we agreed.

Terese So who's the new man in your life, then?

Louise You know, Terese, even you've had men in your life.

Terese What?

Louise Well, you have.

Terese What's that got to do with anything? (*Sudden realisation.*) J.J.?

Louise Erm . . .

Terese This married Russian poet with the prison sentence? It's J.J., isn't it?

Louise Um, yes. (*Quietly.*) I'm sorry.

Terese Listen, you're mistaken. You don't want to go out with J.J. . . . it's . . . er . . .

Louise I know it seems crazy but I've never felt so attracted to someone. Don't ask me to explain it, Terese.

I wish I could, for your sake as well as mine, but . . . J.J.'s so
. . . right.

Terese   When you went home with . . . Did J.J. talk about
. . . J.J.? What I mean is . . . what did J.J. say about . . . talk
about?

Louise   We talked about lots of things, we get on really
well, have done all week. It just gets better and better, in
fact.

Terese   All week? You've been out together all week?

Louise   Pretty much, yeah.

Terese   And you haven't . . . ? J.J. hasn't . . . ? Oh, God, I
could kill . . .

Louise   Me?

Terese   No, J.J.

Terese   You didn't tell Louise!

J.J.   No, I didn't.

Terese   Why not? What the hell do you think you're
playing at? What is it? Fun? Is it some kind of twisted game?
Do you get your kicks out of fooling people, treating them
like idiots? Making them look stupid? I mean, yeah, I
understand the attraction for you. Understand the
harmlessness of you getting your rocks off on some pathetic
fantasy for five minutes. But five minutes! Not carry on with
it, not string her along till she's involved! Louise is my best
friend and you are fucking her around, J.J. . . . . she's going
on about how she likes you and . . . likes you a lot. I had
respect for you, I thought you had more integrity. I mean, I
know it's hard for you, know you're fucked up and
everything – but that's your problem and you should learn
to deal with it without stringing people like Louise along.
You can't use her, it's shitty. Very shitty, J.J.

Slight pause.

J.J.   What are you talking about, Terri?

Terese   You didn't tell Louise.

J.J.   No, I didn't.

Terese   Why?

J.J.   Because she already knew. She's not a moron. But I think you already know that.

———

All three, sitting, serious, awkward. **Terese** *slightly apart, unfriendly.*

Louise   Somebody should try to explain.

Terese   I don't need an explanation.

Louise   It wasn't meant to happen, nobody planned it, it just happened.

Terese   I don't *need* an explanation. And certainly not from you, Louise.

Louise   We need to make friends.

Terese   Do we? Why?

Louise   Because . . . we were friends.

Terese   Were we?

Louise   I thought we were.

Terese   No, not really, you were just somebody I lusted after.

Pause.

J.J.   I don't think Terri needs an explanation.

Louise *looks to* **J.J.**, **Terese** *looks even more miffed.*

J.J.   Just because she fancied you . . . well (*Shrugs*.) doesn't mean you don't have a mind of your own. Doesn't mean you can't choose who you go out with.

Terese   She lied to me.

Louise   No, I didn't. I've never lied to you.

Terese   You told me you were straight.

Louise   I still regard myself as straight.

Terese   Going out with J.J.?

Louise   J.J.'s my boyfriend.

Terese   J.J.'s a woman!

Louise   Maybe to you. But to me and J.J., J.J.'s my boyfriend.

Terese (*moving away*)   Well, then both of you are tapped because as far as I'm concerned you are both lesbians, having a lesbian relationship.

Louise *goes to say something, doesn't, looks at* **J.J.**, *who just shrugs.*

J.J.   If that's how you feel, Terri – who am I . . .

Terese   I thought you were a friend.

J.J.   No, not really, you were just somebody I lusted after.

Terese *and* **Louise** *both look at* **J.J.**

Terese   You fancied me?

Louise   You fancied her?

J.J.   Yeah. But not in a lesbian way.

Louise/Terese   Huh?

J.J.   Well, you're pretty boyish already, why not go the whole hog?

Terese   What do you mean?

J.J.   Be a boy, of course.

Terese (*incredulous*)   You think I should pretend to be a boy?

J.J.   No, be a boy. See, I often think of you, see you as . . . well, fantasise, really. I often fantasise about you and me, you know, a couple of gay guys getting together, somewhere sordid like, I don't know, toilets perhaps, a back alley, Hampstead Heath, Clapham Common, somewhere windy, a nice cool breeze wafting about our naked buttocks while we get together and do all kinds of spunky . . .

Terese (*vehement*)   You are tapped! (*Walks away.*)

J.J.   So, what do you think, Louise?

Louise   You really fantasise about . . . ?

J.J.   Hampstead Heath? In the wind? With my buttocks? I'd catch pneumonia.

Louise   So why did you . . . ?

J.J.   Because she's irritating the fuck out of me.

Louise   So you don't really . . . ?

J.J.   Do I look the type?

Louise *says nothing.*

Terese *with bag of clothes and stuff, various. Begins by trying on girly thing – sort of thing* **Louise** *might wear.*

Terese   'J.J. is my boyfriend, J.J. is my boyfriend' – on Clapham Common with a breeze and buttocks – I'd like to see Louise on Clapham Common, her heels would just stick in the mud! To lose one's best friend is unfortunate, to lose two is . . . a conspiracy. And I've nothing to lose now, except maybe my dignity if I'm rejected. But what's rejected? I've already been rejected. I knew those two should never meet. (*Takes off girly, tries on dildo.*) I remember Karen, big dyke, big diesel dyke, never said anything, rode a motorbike and grunted and cackled like a hyena. Louise was always talking to her. It never occurred to me why – just, what the hell do you talk about to Karen? How the hell can you sustain a conversation when you can't even spell Kawasaki, let alone strip it down. 'J.J. is my boyfriend' – how tapped can you get? Why? Because better jackets. Better jackets. How sure can you be? I've never been that sure, I've never written my own label. Well done you, Louise. Well done, J.J. (*Taking off dildo.*) No. Be a boy. Don't pretend, be. I never realised J.J. had a thing for me. I always thought we were just mates. (*Picks up jacket, but doesn't put it on.*) I should be surprised but . . . I've had men before, was I a lesbian? Was I the same person? Change partners, change labels. Choose a label and come home. And I've stayed home ever since, it's comfortable, it's secure, slippers, cocoa and I'm happy. Was happy. Was happy fancying Louise, though. I wish I'd realised I wasn't man enough for her, wish I'd realised I wasn't butch enough. Better jackets, Karen. (*Puts on the jacket.*) Clapham Common. (*Snorts.*) Tapped!

Louise *agitated.* **J.J.** *sitting leg crossed tight.* **Louise** *arranging* **J.J.***'s leg so it's crossed loose.*

Louise   We should go and see her, apologise.

J.J. (*putting leg back tight*)   We've done nothing wrong.

Louise   She was obviously hurt, obviously upset. (**Louise** *puts* **J.J.***'s leg back loose.*) Maybe you should go, alone, explain about the Hampstead thing. The . . . buttocks and . . . things . . .

J.J.   I've done nothing wrong. (*Puts leg back.*)

Louise   Well, then I should go.

J.J.   You've done nothing . . .

Louise (*losing it*)   Will you stop saying that! She's my best friend, I miss her. I like female company, I like girly stuff – girl talk with girlfriends. (*Makes to put* **J.J.***'s leg back but . . .*)

J.J.   Will you leave my bloody leg alone!

Louise   Well, sit properly, then! Play the game!

J.J. (*standing*)   You know your trouble, Louise? You're so fucking conventional.

Louise   And you know your trouble? You're so . . . so . . .

J.J.   What? Female? Not man enough for you?

Louise   I didn't say that.

J.J.   You don't need to, the position of my leg speaks volumes.

Louise   Well, don't you care?

J.J.   Not particularly. It's like you said – it's just a game.

Louise   No, it's not, far from it.

J.J.   Whatever.

Silence.

J.J. (*finally*)   I'm not trying to be a man, Louise.

Louise   Well, what then?

J.J.   I don't know, whatever comes naturally.

Louise   Well, it doesn't come naturally to me.

J.J.   Obviously.

Louise   So what do you want?

J.J.   I don't know – a cup of tea would be nice.

Louise   From me? What do you want from me?

J.J. *goes to say something.*

Louise   And don't say a cup of tea or I'll brain you.

J.J. *stops going to say something.*

Louise   I'm being serious.

J.J.   I don't know. What do you want?

Louise   I want a really good, loving relationship.

J.J.   And you're not getting it from me?

Louise   Yes. Most of the time I am.

J.J.   But?

Louise   Well . . . what do I tell people?

J.J.   Whatever you like.

Louise   No, you know what I mean. What do I tell myself?

J.J.   That time you said to Terri? You said, so defiantly, 'J.J.'s my boyfriend!' I loved you for that. You weren't quite right, not from my point of view anyway, but I loved the fact that you said it.

Louise   'From your point of view.' But what about from mine?

J.J.   What?

Louise   From my point of view you're my boyfriend.

J.J.   So?

Louise   So I expect you to be it! I expect you to sit like a man, walk like a man, talk like a man, act like a man, make love like a man, be a man.

J.J.   Why don't you just get yourself a man?

Louise   That's not the point and you know it.

Pause.

J.J.   I can't be what I'm not.

Louise   I'm not asking you to be. I just want you to have the courage of your convictions.

J.J.   But they're not my convictions, they're yours. Just because I'm not a woman doesn't mean I have to be pushed, kicking and screaming, into manhood.

Louise   Well, what then?

J.J.   Whatever. Just me being me.

Louise   And that makes me what?

J.J.   Just you being you.

Louise   Which makes us?

J.J.   Us.

Louise   We might as well just be lesbians.

J.J.   Fine. If you have to call it something, call it that.

Louise   So I'm back where I started – hanging around with a woman with a haircut.

J.J.   Is there something wrong with that?

Louise *sighs.*

J.J. (*quietly*)   Obviously.

Terese (*defensively sulky*)   Visited any dark alleys lately? Any toilets?

J.J.   Have you? (*Pause.*) Just where do you get off? You think you have the right to dictate because you're some fully paid-up member of an exclusive little lesbian club and I'm only provisional? Because I'm marginal, a fringe member?

Terese   It has nothing to do with that.

J.J.   Doesn't it?

Terese   I don't care what your sexual proclivities are.

J.J.   So long as you can name and shame them.

Terese   That is unfair. I have never questioned anybody's . . .

J.J.   Oh, you pretend not to. You pretend to be the great liberal, just as long as you're on top, as long as you're winning. What gives you the right to tell me and Lou what kind of relationship we're having? Or what kind of relationship we should be having?

Terese   It has nothing to do with your relationship.

J.J.   Doesn't it?

Terese   I was hurt, upset, jealous. I wanted it to be me. I wanted to be the one to show her. Anyway, don't you come accusingly at me. You're the one who won.

J.J.   I didn't 'win' anything.

Terese   I didn't see you walking away empty-handed.

J.J.   She's not a trophy, you know.

Terese   Isn't she? Isn't that what you thought? I mean why, all of a sudden, did you become so gung-ho over her?

Silence. A little less aggression.

Terese   Anyway, what have you got that I haven't got?

J.J.   Better jackets?

Terese *half smiles ruefully.*

Pause.

Terese   I was just so . . . so . . . Ugh! She said she wasn't a lesbian. She's always said she wasn't a lesbian.

J.J.   She's not.

Terese   Yeah, yeah, all right, whatever you want to call it. It's still deep down, bottom line, two women. Whatever's in your head, whatever, but anatomically – two women.

J.J.   Yeah.

Terese   Well, then.

J.J.   Maybe it's just a question of words. Nouns. Labels.

Terese   Words. It's only words – a rose by any other name blah, blah, blah.

J.J.   If you feel like a rose you call yourself a rose. If you don't feel like a rose you say nothing and other people call you a rose. And then you get grief for arguing because you don't feel like a fucking rose in the first place.

Terese   What?

J.J.   You and Lou have so much in common. Male, female, gay, straight. Boxed, labelled, bored. Clowns to the left of me, jokers to the right.

Terese   Am I the joker or the clown?

J.J.   You're the typical lesbian. (*Sings.*) Here I am stuck in the middle with you.

Terese *kisses* **J.J.***'s forehead.*

J.J. (*quietly*)   You think this is funny? You think this is a game? You think it's just a question of sticking a pair of socks down your knickers and taking the piss? You have no idea, really, no idea of what it's like to be unable to move sometimes, to have to plan the day down to the last detail so as to try and move through it with the least amount of fuss. Every day somebody wants to know what gender I am. Every day somebody wants to know where I fit in. Every day somebody wants to argue with me about womanhood or manhood or feminism or lesbianism or . . . treachery. Treachery's the favourite. Everybody wants to know where I stand, or what fence I sit on, or what kind of bed I've made for myself. If I acknowledge one half of me, I silence the other half of me. I can't move. I don't know where to move to. But I know one thing: if I had a choice . . . I'd choose it. Are we friends or what?

Terese (*sighs*)   Yeah, we're friends.

J.J.   Despite all the deeply wounding things you said about me?

Terese   What deeply wounding . . . ?

J.J.   Okay, I'll take that as an apology.

Terese   None intended, I'm sure.

J.J.   She doesn't understand me.

Terese   Uh-oh, you'll be calling her your wife in a minute, then suggesting I become your bit on the side.

J.J.   You know what I mean.

Terese   No, I don't. Do you understand yourself?

J.J.   No.

Terese   Well, then, why should anybody else?

J.J.   True.

Terese   God, it's cold, isn't it.

J.J.   What?

Terese   Out here, in no-man's-land, cold. (*Puts on jacket from previous scene.*)

J.J. (*amused*)   You stole my jacket.

Terese   I borrowed your jacket.

J.J. (*nonplussed*)   Why?

Terese   Because you've got great jackets. Because I was jealous. Because I like pot-pourris. Because I liked kissing in the lesbian corner. What would you prefer? Hampstead Heath or a toilet?

Uncertain pause from **J.J.**

J.J.   That was a joke.

Terese   Everything always is with you. So?

J.J.   So?

Terese   So? Hampstead Heath or a toilet?

J.J.   A dark alley. With no names, no labels and no genders.

Terese   Like I already said: no-*man*'s-land.

J.J. No-man's-land is good

Beginning the sex. Music – something clichéd like 'Relax'.

Terese You're not so different from me and Louise, you know. In fact, I'd go so far as to say you're quite *typical*, really.

J.J. Speaking of Louise . . .

Terese Let's not speak of Louise just now, let's just hope she . . . gets a headache.

J.J. So what does this make us?

Terese Just us.

J.J. *and* **Terese** *getting well into whatever.*

Sodom

Lot's Wife   In a nutshell: Two angels arrive at Sodom and everybody's gay except Lot and his family. (Imagine San Fransisco on a hot day.) And all the gay guys say, 'We want to fuck the angels!' And Lot says, 'No, you can't fuck the angels.' Lot gets saved, Sodom gets destroyed, and the angels go to Gomorrah. End of story.

Doom   What are you thinking? Sex? Hot, rampant, reckless sex? Buggery, sodomy, fellatio, anything you like, anything you can? Yes, I'm sure that's what you're thinking. Okay, let's go with it: my hair plastered to my head with sweat and flying spunk and countless oily hands grabbing at my body, my mouth. My eyes, open to naked, writhing bodies massed around me, or closed in helpless physical, pulsating, orgasmic bliss. The heat air-drying the spittle of licks, kisses, bites on my neck, chest, face, stomach, legs, back, arse, groin. My mouth licking kissing biting sucking the cock that's nearest, next to me, within reach. Who are they? I don't know. What are they? I don't care. It's irrelevant. What counts is the feeling, what counts is the event. Drugs? Yes, we use drugs. Our minds sneaking away, reason erased, crawling with passion, wading through bodies. My only rational thought: don't come yet, don't exhaust the possibility, don't collapse wasted and spent and sleepy. My cock, sliding into hard calloused hands, open salivating mouths, tight, wet and sweaty, half-greased arses. Everything dripping, everything sticky and sliding from someone else's juice. Is that what you want? Is that what you expected . . . But . . . hard calloused hands? I said that, didn't I? I said hard calloused hands. Because we work. We farm and labour and build. In the valley, a beautiful, fertile valley. Shall I tell you about our politics? Shall I tell you about our religion? Nobody's ever too keen to ask about that. Nobody's quite so keen to know about our humanity. Just the sex. Everybody banging on about the sex.

Lot   Abraham just got this bee in his bonnet about one God – his God. Well, I'm just starting out so what do I know? So we travel about a lot and he's very successful –

we're picking up people, servants, cattle, land. Doing all right, doing more than all right. This one-God business seems to be working, so I'm not arguing, right? Well, I wouldn't be arguing anyway, because I was part of it and it felt *great*. Can you imagine? Being part of it, a big band – and we were getting *huge* – and we didn't particularly stop. We just went from place to place and sort of . . . took over. They could see us coming, couldn't miss us, kicking up the dust like a huge cloud of rolling thunder as we approached, awe-inspiring before we even got there. And then of course the sight of us, hundreds of us, herds of people, herds of animals. Well, that many people can't be wrong. So, one God, our God, our own special God, just for us, people loved it, people were falling over themselves to join, because think about it, the sight of us, we couldn't fail, our God couldn't fail. And basically we just shared their fields. They joined the band and we took the fields.

Doom   We wouldn't give our fields. We wouldn't join the band. We've been subjugated before and do you know what? It wasn't much fun. Besides we're quite happy with the Gods we've got. And it's Gods – not God. Not one God, that's not us. That's your cult, and that cult belongs outside our world.

Lot   My cult?

Doom   Yeah, your cult.

Lot   You are the cult.

Doom   No you are. You're the biggest cult I've ever seen.

Lot   Is that some kind of pathetic joke?

Doom *laughs*.

Lot   You should watch your mouth.

Doom   What's wrong with my mouth?

Lot   You say what's on your mind.

Doom   Yeah? So?

Lot   Well, don't. That way trouble lies.

Doom (*shrugs*)   Oh I think we're all aware of that. But one God? It's a cult. The One-God Cult. It's a novel idea. Inspires a certain reassurance in its simplicity, because one God means one idea.

Lot   And One God means one way of looking.

Doom   One God means one rigid, set, tied, gagged and bound set of rules, regulations, dos and don'ts, haves and have nots. And who's the best?

Lot   No competition.

Doom   Which God gives you the best, what you want, what you need?

Lot   No choice.

Doom   Which God suits you?

Lot   Only one.

Doom   Lot's Uncle Abraham is some kind of big prophet – isn't that right, Lot?

Lot   That's right, Doom.

Doom   He's told me about it but I don't really get it – either the concept or the point. Lot was brought up by his uncle and aunt, fanatical about this one God apparently, whatever that's worth. Lot lives just outside of town, he introduced me to his tribe. I was polite but terrified – I've never seen so much wealth. Don't know what he wants with it, mind you, he's always hanging around here.

Lot   So then God told Abraham to go to Egypt.

Doom   How did he do that? How did he tell him?

Lot   In a dream. And we went, en masse. It was a bad year for the harvest, well, in fact, there wasn't one, wasn't a harvest. Crop failure all round, couldn't feed the people, couldn't feed the animals, so . . . now most people would have panicked, most people would have split up the tribe, concentrated on the immediate family and to hell with the rest. But not my uncle, or rather not this God. And things just got better. This God, you see, he knew what was what. And off we went to Egypt. Anyway, so my uncle said to my aunt, 'Pretend you're my sister', because Abraham was sure he'd be killed by the Egyptians. He thought Sarah was so good-looking that they'd want her and have to kill him to have her. They did want her, he was right about that, my aunt is a looker, no doubt about that. Next thing I know she's with the Pharaoh. And my uncle . . .

Doom   With the Pharaoh?

Lot   Yeah, and my uncle as head of the tribe . . .

Doom   With the Pharaoh? You mean screwing the Pharaoh?

Lot   Sort of. And my uncle as head of the tribe . . .

Doom   Screwing the Pharaoh?

Lot   Yeah, it was necessary. So my uncle as head of the tribe is being showered with even more stuff . . .

Doom   Necessary? To screw the Pharaoh?

Lot   Yeah – showered with more animals, more slaves, gold, more wealth.

Doom   Simple as that, it was necessary to screw the Pharaoh, so she screwed the Pharaoh.

Lot   Will you stop saying that.

Doom   I'm sorry but I'm enjoying it. It feels nice to say 'screwing the Pharaoh'. It sounds sexy and squishy and, dare I say it, almost depraved. Almost reminiscent of Sodom in fact: the rich exotic foreigner, his fingers probing, exploring, his huge throbbing erect cock thrusting forward, delving deeply into the warm, moist pudendum of our hero's wife. While our hero, strangely aloof, and ever so slightly cowardly, looks on.

Lot   Abraham could've been killed! Don't you understand that? Have you any idea what a perilous position he was in?

Doom   Couldn't his God save him?

Lot   God did save him! His power is awesome. The Pharaoh got ill. And a lot of those around the Pharaoh got the same thing.

Doom   The Pharaoh got ill? How do you mean ill?

Lot   You know, ill, sores and pustules and . . . stuff.

Doom   Sort of VD ill, do you mean?

Lot   Power of God ill, I mean.

Doom   Power of God?

Lot   My uncle said that was the power of our God and who was I to doubt it?

Doom   Who were you indeed.

Lot   So we left.

Doom   As you would – pretty damn quick, I imagine, I mean, giving the Pharaoh V . . .

Lot   You should watch your mouth.

Doom   What's wrong with my mouth?

Lot   You say what's on your mind.

Doom   Yeah? So?

Lot   Well, don't. That way trouble lies.

Doom   I think we've said all this before.

Lot   Anyway, we decided to split up. Well, arguments, you know, there were arguments. Things had gotten too big. Not just between me and Abraham but also among some of my people and some of his. And space, there was a lack of space. So I took a bunch of people and animals and stuff, and headed down to Sodom.

Doom   Ta da!

Angel   Sex. Homosexual sex. Dirty, disgusting, depraved.
Penises. Erect. Rampant. Spunk-filled, spunk-fuelled. Huge,
engorged monstrosities spewing forth their hot, molten lava
of lust. Wading, knee-deep, up to their necks, up to their
ears, way over their heads in the depths of depravity. The
citizens of Sodom . . .

Lot   There was a spot of trouble. Not at Sodom,
somewhere else, but the guy who was causing the trouble,
Chedorlaomer, he'd given Doom and the boys some grief
before.

Doom   Subjugated, as I said, for twelve long years. In the
thirteenth year we . . . well, thirteen, unlucky for some.
Unlucky for Chedorlaomer.

Lot   So revenge and whatnot, everybody decided to help
out, so off they went. I went too, don't ask me why. Well,
okay, I'm living here, right, and these people are okay, not
my tribe, not what I'm used to, but I've had no trouble and
they're all right, they're okay, friendly, neighbours. You've
got to be neighbourly. So off we all went to fight this battle.

Doom   They busted our arses. We got well and truly
routed.

Lot   I sent a message to my uncle Abraham. I didn't know
what else to do. They took all my stuff, cattle, slaves, gold,
everything. I'd never been on the losing side before.

Angel   We're all for having friends, all for being
neighbourly, but what the hell were you thinking of? What
the hell were you doing there? We are missionaries, we have
a reputation. Abraham's got an empire, converts in very
high places, how do you suppose they would react if news of
this . . . this . . . your shenanigans got out? Lot, you didn't
split up for this, didn't come down to Sodom for this.
You've been educated, you know about God. You know
about his power, it's your mission to explain. You had
wealth, head of your tribe, you had cattle, you had slaves,

servants – you were well on the way to taking over that land, the whole of the valley should have been yours. Your career path was mapped out, don't screw it up.

Doom (*to* **Angel**)   Did you know that the penis is not just an exterior organ? That it in fact continues deep inside the body, running parallel and adjacent to the anal canal? So, therefore, with the actual organ being so long, the only way to experience a total penis experience is if somebody inserts his penis into your anus, and then you put your penis into a hand, mouth, vagina or another arse. It's a kind of all bases covered, complete massage, wraparound experience. We're still not sure if that's the male equivalent to the clitoris, but we reckon it comes pretty damn close.

Angel   Infidels. Godless, ignorant, unchanged idol worshippers. It's worse than I thought, there's a genuine moral danger here, these people are depraved. Lot, you have to move.

Lot   I don't want to. This valley is a garden of Eden, and I can still convert them.

Angel   Well, then, you need help. (*Gesture introduces* **Lot's Wife**.)

Lot's Wife   One God means one idea. And one God means one way of looking. One God means one rigid, set, tied, gagged and bound set of rules, regulations, dos and don'ts, haves and have nots. And who's the best? No competition. Which God gives you the best, what you want, what you need? No choice. Which God suits you? Only one. So you suit the God. Bend and change and suffer to suit the God. Hide and hush up and cover up and stand still, buried, under a stone. The God stone. The weight. (*Pause.*) Land, basically. What we're talking about is land, I'm sure of it. Oh, I do believe that Abraham believes. I do believe he believes in his God. He believes in his God with a passion that's . . . frightening, but . . . he also wants the land.

Lot I was supposed to come here and take over. When we split up and I chose the valley, the understanding was that I convert the valley. Sodom, Gomorrah, Admah, Zeboiim, Bela. And maybe I still believe in one God, I don't know, but . . . I love this valley. These people, the people of Sodom, they've worked this land – they love this land. And at first, oh yes I could see my mistake, I could see what a den of iniquity I'd landed myself in . . .

Lot's Wife The actual den of iniquity was two doors down from Lot, so it wasn't too much of an effort to saddle up the old erection and mosey on over.

Lot What are you saying?

Lot's Wife *shrugs*.

Lot I couldn't believe their lifestyles, couldn't believe their disgusting practices – sex and drugs and orgies and . . . sex with anybody, anything went, whatever turned them on. So different from before, so different from life with Abraham. And at first I thought I must tell them about God, must instruct them, tell them the truth, the way, bring some sort of order to this chaos, but . . . then I started seeing the love, the respect, community. Started questioning . . .

Lot's Wife Power. Men at the top, women at the bottom, slaves below that. This one God is a male God, he works in the male way. Wealth, power, position. Hierarchy. God speaks to Abraham, Abraham speaks to us. I lived with him, I know. If you argue with Abraham you're arguing with God, if you disagree with Abraham you're disagreeing with God. You might as well just cut your tongue out and stamp it into the earth. You can say nothing. If something goes right, God did it. If something goes wrong, God did it to punish you. Whichever way you move it's either out of your hands or you're to blame. And women. Women are so low. Women are not like God, they have no voice, they have no authority. There is no Goddess to appeal to, no other God to curry favour with. Just this one, this one God, and he does not like you. You are doomed, you are damned just for being born. Why? Because Abraham says so.

Angel   They disgust me. Perverts the lot of them. There is no respect in what they do, no restraint, no love. They abuse themselves and abuse each other, and then ask us to accept that wallowing around in a cesspit of their own making is natural. Natural. Nothing natural in what they do. It is disgusting, depraved. These queers will have to go.

Lot   I knew there'd be trouble, saw it coming. I tried to get the angels into the house as quick as possible but they'd already been seen, already been spotted. And by the sudden flurry of activity, the scampering, whispering and running around, I knew they'd do something stupid. I do love Doom and the boys, but really, they are getting paranoid. If they'd gone quietly to their houses, kept their heads down, we might have avoided trouble, the angels could have come, twiddled their thumbs and then left again. As it is, God knows what's going to happen – and I mean that literally. I've lived with Abraham and I know what he's like. I blame myself. If I hadn't decided to stay here maybe they'd have been left in peace, maybe they'd just have been tolerated as the happy hippies they are.

Doom   We knew who they were. Bloody fanatics, can smell them a mile away. What annoys me, what *really* annoys me is, okay, whatever they want to believe is fine by me, live and let live, but do *they* see it like that? So, they come, to *our* town, to *our* manor. Then, they try to tell *us* how to live our lives. Well, I mean, cheek or what? So I was annoyed. Too bloody right I was annoyed. I thought all right, okay, you know who we are, you've heard all the rumours, listened to all the gossip, made up your own bloody minds with no thought – *no thought.* So all right, okay, if that's what you're expecting, if that's what you expect of us, we'll give it to you. Too bloody right we'll give it to you, in spades. Because, these fanatics, there's no reasoning with them, they just simply won't be happy till everybody's a mirror image of them. And quite frankly I couldn't give a stuff. I'm not interested. Not in them, or their God – *I don't want to join.*

Lot's Wife   There is no choice now, many gods and goddesses mean many choices, I don't want to lose that. I have a choice now. I have a voice. Maybe nobody is listening, but then I'm not being told either. Here I am not kicked to the floor with my nose rubbed in the dirt because I have sexual desires. The same sexual desires that Abraham speaks of, the sexual desires of Eve. Eve, punished for being a woman. Created by God and then punished for being created. Created with sexual desire and then punished for her sexual desire. There is no such punishment here. In Sodom sexual desire is worshipped, celebrated, encouraged.

Doom   Agents provocateurs, trying to look menacing, trying to look threatening . . . no, sexy. They look *so sexy*. We knew what they were doing though, we knew what they wanted, trying to wind us up, trying to provoke. Okay, all right, you think we're raging sexual deviants – then we'll give you raging sexual deviancy, we decided. There was a bunch of us, it was supposed to be a laugh, a joke. 'Come on, let's fuck!' we shouted. 'Come on, Lot, who're your friends, bring them out, let's have them!' They didn't think it was funny. Poor old Lot he was panicking, trying to lock his door. Well, so naturally we tried to bang it down, right? Just as a joke, we weren't really going to fuck his friends – well, not unless they wanted to anyway. Angels he said they were. *Angels? Angels?* Oh please! Excuse me, but I can recognise militia at a hundred paces, even if they are dressed up sexy and posing. And believe me, these guys were sexy and posing!

Lot's Wife   If a woman has a child, all the men are fathers. If a woman has no child, she is a mother to all the other children. We are all family, all tribe.

Doom   Well, I suppose things *did* get a bit out of hand – no sense of humour either, these people, can't take a joke, you know, they say, 'God's not funny,' well, excuse me, but

I saw them coming, I've seen from the outside, bloody hysterical, if you ask me. Not that I was laughing at the time, well, not when things got out of hand, just got bloody angry then. But it started off as a joke, sort of. Anyway, I don't know what they did, what they used on us but, blimey it hurt. Couldn't see a thing, tears streaming down my face. I thought my eyes were on fire – some sort of smoke, I don't know. They'd obviously come prepared anyway. Some of the others thought we'd played right into their hands but I don't know, what do they want to get at us for? We're not hurting anybody.

Angel God's power is awesome, God's power is everywhere. God's power is bigger than you and bigger than all your gods rolled into one. And God will cut you down as easily as clicking his fingers.

Doom Yeah, right, because I'm doing things with my penis that he doesn't want me to – or more to the point: why is Lot still here?

Angel You should watch your mouth.

Doom What's wrong with my mouth?

Angel You say what's on your mind.

Doom Yeah? So?

Angel Well, don't. That way trouble lies.

Doom Fancy a fuck?

Angel You're dead!

Doom I know.

Lot You shouldn't have done that, Doom.

Doom I know that too.

Lot's Wife We are all family, all tribe. Well, not us, not quite, but we were getting there. Two of my daughters belong, and I have hopes for my other two. Lot, he is divided, worried, fearful. Maybe Abraham's God is right,

maybe Abraham's God is real – the one true God. It worked
for Lot, for a while. And why not, he had everything –
power, position, wealth. With Abraham he was important.
Here, he is just one of the guys – and a foolish one at that,
he holds no high position here.

Doom   Did you know that the penis is not just an exterior
organ? That it in fact continues deep inside the body,
running parallel and adjacent to the anal canal?

Lot (*pleading with* **Doom**)   Take my daughters instead,
they're virgins.

Angel   They think they're clever, think this God is like
their gods. Think it's a hope-and-a-prayer god. But I've
seen, I know. I've seen the signs in the mountains, felt the
rumble under the earth.

Lot's Wife   If a woman has a child, all the men are
fathers. If a woman has no child, she is a mother to all the
other children. We are all family, all tribe.

Doom   So, therefore, with the actual organ being so long,
the only way to experience a total penis experience is if
somebody inserts his penis into your anus, and then you put
your penis into a hand, mouth, vagina or another arse. I
have a set of beliefs as long as your arm. I have gods. I have
gods who've shown me awe-inspiring cosmic things.

Lot   My daughters are young, healthy, willing to do . . .
whatever.

Lot's Wife   All the men are fathers.

Angel   Absolutely no sense of respect, dignity,
responsibility . . .

Doom   Things that would make your mind explode. (*To*
Angel.) Your man isn't the only guy to have dreams, you
know.

Lot's Wife   Paternity.

Angel   God knows I'm a tolerant person, but some things are cancerous, some people are beyond redemption.

Lot's Wife   Inheritance, dynasty, passing the mantle, maintaining the reins of power.

Angel   Their message is godlessness, their message is evil.

Lot   These people are not joking, Doom, this is the new order.

Doom   But the most cosmic thing I've been shown is the human. The human body, human mind, human emotions. And the greatest pleasure is pleasure. It's a kind of all bases covered, complete massage, wraparound experience. We're still not sure if that's the male equivalent to the clitoris, but we reckon it comes pretty damn close.

Lot   Enough, stop it, you're asking for trouble.

Doom   No I'm not, I'm being honest. And I know exactly what's at stake.

Lot   Do you?

Doom   Oh yeah, but we don't want your daughters. We don't want virgins pushed at us to appease your panic.

Lot   If a woman has a child, all the men are fathers. Inheritance, dynasty, passing the mantle, maintaining the reins of power.

Angel   There is freedom in God. There is freedom in putting your life, your soul, your destiny in the hands of the one true God. And isn't he protecting us? Isn't he winning? Whose lives are on shaky ground? Not ours. We can't be defeated. If the truth is so obvious, if the truth is so blatant and it takes the destruction of a few non-believers to prove it, then that's what needs to be done. And I'm more than happy to do it.

Lot   We were told to get out, we were told the whole place was going to blow, the whole area. They told us to run and not look back. My wife looked back.

A giant, cosmic, pyrotechnic explosion. Something never before achieved in the history of British, penniless, tatty, gaffer-taped theatre.

Lot's Wife   Doom! (*Becoming a pillar of salt.*)

Angel   *The Lord rained upon Sodom and upon Gomorrah brimstone and fire from the Lord out of heaven.*
And he overthrew those cities, and all the plain, and all the inhabitants of the cities, and that which grew upon the ground.
But Lot's wife looked back from behind him, and she became a pillar of salt.

Doom   I don't believe in your God. I have my own gods. But our greatest crime is our lack of hypocrisy. Our reputation damns us, honesty damns us.

Angel   Sex. Homosexual sex. Dirty, disgusting, depraved. Penises. Erect. Rampant. Spunk-filled, spunk-fuelled. Huge, engorged monstrosities spewing forth their hot, molten lava of lust. Wading, knee-deep, up to their necks, up to their ears, way over their heads in the depths of depravity. The citizens of Sodom . . .

Doom   Inhabitants of a fertile valley, surrounded by mountains, volcanic mountains. Huge, engorged monstrosities spewing forth their hot, molten lava of destruction. Wading, knee-deep, up to our necks, blah blah blah. (*Dying.*)

Angel   *But the men of Sodom were wicked and sinners before the Lord exceedingly.*

Lot   We were told to get out, we were told the whole place was going to blow, the whole area. They told us to run and not look back. My wife looked back.

Angel   She was told not to look.

Lot   She looked.

Angel   What you going to say?

Lot   Nothing.

Angel   What you going to say?

Lot   It was necessary.

Angel   What you going to say?

Lot   It was meant, it was holy, it was righteous.

Angel   And your aunt Sarah is with child.

Lot's Wife   Doom!

Angel   In a nutshell: Two angels arrive at Sodom and everybody's gay except Lot and his family. (Imagine San Fransisco on a hot day.) And all the gay guys say, 'We want to fuck the angels!' And Lot says, 'No, you can't fuck the angels.' Lot gets saved, Sodom gets destroyed, and the angels go to Gomorrah. End of story. Hopefully.

The actors clear up the mess of destruction.

Doom   But Lot actually told the gay guys not to fuck the angels but to fuck his virginal, young daughters instead. And for this Lot is a Christian role model, to be held up and shook in the face of itinerants who want to have good sex with consenting partners. And then, after Lot's wife has been turned into a pillar of salt (by God, conveniently!), just because she turned round because she couldn't remember if she'd turned the gas off or not, both Lot's daughters get pregnant. By Lot! Incest with God's blessing? Is this something Christians want to brag about? Although apparently Lot knew nothing about it, so that's all right then. He had too much wine, couldn't remember fucking his daughters. Excuse me, but if you've had too much wine to remember fucking your daughters, then you've had too much wine to get it up enough to fuck your daughters in the first place!

Lot's Wife   Lot's wife.

Doom   What about her?

Lot's Wife   *But Lot's wife looked back from behind him, and she became a pillar of salt.*

Doom   Pillar of salt? What's that mean 'pillar of salt'?

Lot's Wife   No bloody idea, but Sodom was by the salt sea.

Lot   The Dead Sea. The amazing thing about the Dead Sea is the density of salt in it. If you drop anything in it, it's instantly encrusted with salt, frozen and preserved at the same time. Nothing can live in it.

Doom   So she took a dive?

Angel   In a manner of speaking.

Lot's Wife   Not a dive. A searing insight. Everything became clear. A big tidal wave of understanding engulfed her. Knowledge, guilt and rage washing over her, like a mass explosion . . .

Lot   Yeah, there could have been a tidal wave – or an earthquake, because we're in earthquake territory here. Very volatile country, geographically speaking. Tidal wave, earthquake, volcano. A big volcano exploding with lava and salt. Can you imagine that? A mass wave of lava and salt crashing towards you, smashing into you, washing over you . . .

Lot's Wife   Totally fixing her into a petrified pose of utter despair as she turned for one last second to say a final goodbye to friends, family, the people she loved and lived with for . . .

Angel   Oh, do shut up, woman!

Lot's Wife   This was a desperately tragic event!

Angel   *But the men of Sodom were wicked and sinners before the Lord exceedingly.* This was retribution from God, visited upon disgusting men with disgusting practices.

Doom   How very convenient for the pushing, jostling machinations of the political string pullers of the time.

Lot   But what's Aunt Sarah being pregnant got to do with it?

Lot's Wife   It means it was all for nothing. You weren't that important after all.

Doom   Inheritance, dynasty, passing the mantle, maintaining the reigns of power. Fatherhood, basically.

Lot's Wife   It's what I was trying to say.

Lot   And one God?

Lot's Wife   A row of cabbages.

Angel   Exactly, dear lady, a row of cabbages – all looking the same, acting the same, being the same.

Lot's Wife   And God made everything . . .

Angel   So you lose and I win every time.

Doom   So God made me.

Angel   Old chestnut.

Doom   And the clitorises and penises that run the length of anal canals and orgasms and the intoxicating smell of sex and sweat and the feel of flesh rubbing against flesh and even . . . even – and you've got to agree – the incredibly pleasant sensation of crapping. Well, when you haven't got piles anyway.

Lot   There's no need for this, you're already dead.

Doom   I know, but I enjoy it.

Angel   Obviously. A mouth and mind like a sewer.

Doom   Sewers are useful. They keep the smell of civilisation above ground while the real shit's happening below the surface.

Angel   Below the surface I can live with.

Doom   Hypocrite.

Interval.

Toolly   From my house, from the attic bedroom you can
see the farmhouse. You can't see inside obviously, but you
can see activity round about. You can see the farmyard, the
outbuildings, the fields, see the people coming and going.
Hippies. Dirty, wasted, pathetic hippies. They appalled me.
If you look through binoculars you can see them quite
clearly, see what they're wearing, see the expressions on
their faces, see what they're doing. Echo. I first saw Echo
through binoculars. His trousers were all saggy and baggy
and ripped. He kept hitching them up as he fed the
chickens. He wasn't wearing anything else, apart from
boots, hardly ever does. His body was brown and lean,
muscular but not excessively so. Fit. Working fit. Farm fit.
I once watched them getting busted through binoculars. I
laughed. The police were rough, disgusted, disdainful – it
was quite obvious there was no lawyer in the house. Good,
I thought – hippies, drunk, drugged up, loved up, fucked up
– serves them right – 'Get a bloody job, you dropouts!'
When I moved into my house, Havenwood, I had assumed,
as anyone would, that my neighbours were farmers, that the
farmhouse was inhabited by a couple of interbred ruddy-
faced middle-aged peasants presiding over a huge brood of
interbred ruddy-faced smaller peasants. That their lives
consisted of milking cows, tramping around in shit and
muttering moronic, country-folk-quaint sayings while
leaning on a gate chewing straw. In other words, nothing to
bother with. Apart, of course, from the worry of theft. My
house was like a fortress, state of the art. CCTV, automatic
electronic shutters, infrared trip lights, high gates, high walls
and Dobermanns. The binoculars I'd bought to go hunting.
New money joining old money – I was quite excited.
I watched Echo having sex through binoculars. They were
round the side of the cowshed. They'd finished milking,
finished mucking out, now they were chatting, him and a
girl. She knelt, gave him a blow job, I masturbated.
When I first arrived I counted about twenty-five of them,
various ages. Now there are sixty-eight – not counting Lydia
and myself.

Echo   Hippies, everybody calls us hippies, or anarchists.
We're not either, we're not anything. I don't even know
what a hippie is. And from what I can gather an anarchist is
somebody who goes against something. We don't go against
anything, we're just living our own lives in our own way.
Toolly's Uncle Polter is some kind of big businessman – isn't
that right, Toolly?

Toolly   That's right, Echo.

Echo   He's told me about it but I don't really get it –
either the concept or the point. Toolly was brought up by
his uncle and aunt, dripping with money apparently,
whatever that's worth. Toolly's got a Porsche but he hardly
ever drives it any more. He drove me once, into town. I
laughed my head off but I was terrified – it's not the same as
being in the back of a police van, you can see out and I
thought the trees were going to hit us.

Toolly   I was successful. Incredibly successful – well, at
least Polter was and I was part of the firm. I was twenty-
four, Thatcherite, a Porsche, several noughts in the old bank
account, a mass of girlfriends and, now, the proud owner of
Havenwood. Well, proud till I bought the binoculars and
saw my neighbours. Echo. At first I hated him. Hated all of
them. Despised, abhorred, loathed. Dirty, unwashed, wasted
hippies. Had I known . . . had I known my neighbours,
bringing down property prices, engaged in immoral,
disgusting depraved practices. Running around, screeching,
naked, cackling like hyenas – crazy. Had I known, then . . .

Echo   We're not hippies.

Toolly   Then. In the beginning.

Echo   We weren't hippies then either.

Toolly   I'm just telling the story so people get the idea: the
clothes, the hair, the lifestyle. You weren't your average
everyday run-of-the-mill farming types. Anyway, your
parents were hippies.

Echo   No they weren't.

Toolly   They set the whole thing up in the sixties.

Echo   Seventies, actually.

Toolly   Nineteen seventy – that's late sixties by anybody's standards. And they were into sex, drugs, rock and roll, peace and love and self-sufficiency – which is hippies!

Polter   It's a cult. He's living next door to a cult. What possessed him to live there God only knows, I thought he was sensible, I thought he had more sense than that. We took him in, my wife and I, sent him to the best schools, decent education, decent upbringing. Treated him like a son, like the son we never had, never could have. Took him under my wing after university. You need allies in business, need to watch your back, surround yourself with trustworthy cohorts and underlings. If you can't trust your own nephew, who can you trust? I mean, I'm all for kids having fun, sowing a few wild oats – even the odd experiment with a line of coke – well, it's just youthful high spirits, isn't it? In my day it was pot. But basically, deep down, Toolly is sensible. He knows the way the world turns, knows what success is and what it can do for you. He used to be ambitious. I thought we'd brought him up successfully.

Echo   I was born here. Grew up here. I know who my natural mom is, but my natural dad could be any number of guys. Toolly was obsessed with it to begin with, obsessed with parentage, it never occurred to me, and even now I still wonder why he wants to know, why he tries to work out who I look like. All the people here are my family. Even Toolly's become a brother. Till I met Toolly I'd never been off the farm, never felt the need to. Okay, I'm thick – it never occurred to me that there was an 'off the farm'. Mind you, having been out, I still can't quite see the point. I prefer knowing everybody, although it was nice to see the world. Here, I'm happy here, got everything I need, people, food, clothes, home, fun. Outside, in the world, they've got police. Police and crime and pollution and clocks. The police come

from time to time – never met such a bunch of miserable
fuckers in my life. They used to scare me. They just irritate
me now.

Toolly   It turned into an obsession. The binoculars. Then
one night there was a party. It was summer, hot. They'd
been harvesting, spent the days harvesting, the nights
partying. I watched Echo having sex. There was a lot of sex,
wasn't just Echo. But this particular night, this particular
party Echo was with a guy. They were both so obviously
stoned, everybody was. Everybody outside, spilling out of
the farmhouse on a hot summer's evening, laughing,
drinking, smoking, enjoyment. No rules. There seemed to
be no rules at the farm. No sense of decency, no morals, no
fear that anyone might be watching. Echo having sex with a
guy. Echo giving the blow job this time, Echo kneeling.
Then standing, turning, both of them naked, the guy behind
wrapping his arms around Echo's chest, wrapping his hand
round Echo's cock, his own cock buried deep inside Echo,
Echo leaning forward slightly, holding on to the side of the
house. A gram or two of charlie. Nothing wrong, weird,
untoward about going round and trying to score some coke.
Nothing wrong with enquiring, asking, introducing myself.

Echo   We got busted. About half an hour after Toolly
arrived the police steamed in.

Toolly   I phoned Uncle Polter. I didn't know what else to
do. I'd never been arrested before.

Polter   I'm all for having friends, I'm all for having fun,
but what the hell were you thinking of? What the hell were
you doing there? We are decent people, we have a
reputation. I have friends, clients in very high places, how
do you suppose they would react if news of this . . . this . . .
your shenanigans got out? Toolly, we didn't bring you up
for this, didn't bring you up to mix with people like this.
You went to proper schools, expensive schools. You've got
good table manners, you know how to behave at dinner
parties. Your aunt and I go to church every Sunday, we mix

with decent people, people with connections. You have contacts, the right suits, the right look, the right accent – you're well on the way to a comfortable, cosseted life with a more than decent early pension. Your career path is mapped out, don't screw it up!

Echo (*to* **Polter**)   Did you know that the penis is not just an exterior organ? It in fact continues deep inside the body, running parallel and adjacent to the anal canal. So the only way to experience a total penis experience is if somebody inserts his penis into your anus, and you insert your penis . . .

Polter   Satanists. Black magic devil worshippers. It's worse than I thought, there's a genuine moral danger here, these people are depraved. Toolly, you have to move.

Toolly   I don't want to. I've just had my kitchen completely redesigned.

Polter   Well, then, you need help. (*Gesture introduces* **Lydia**.)

Lydia   I hope it's a minimalist kitchen, I adore minimalist kitchens. A completely chrome space with just a bowl of oranges, strategically placed . . . do you employ a cleaner?

Toolly   Lydia I adored. She was tall, beautiful, sophisticated. My friends lusted after her, Lydia's friends lusted after her, Echo lusted after her. We held dinner parties with all our 'right' friends and talked about all the 'right' things, which mostly entailed bitching to boredom, then snorting coke. Coke incidentally which I *didn't* get from the farm. They didn't do coke. They did opium, cannabis and magic mushrooms – it's what grew. But then Lydia got pregnant and we got married. We hired part of a stately home for the reception – and the photos and video.

Lydia   I can't manage I can't cope. The nanny's useless, can't even speak English. She spends all day on the phone chatting to friends, the kids don't eat properly, she feeds them junk food. Have you see what's in the freezer! Processed. Everything! I would stay at home, bring them up

properly but there's no kudos in it, I would be despised.
Besides which I'd go mad, talking to nobody but the
mothers at the school gates, standing like a cow getting fat
and frumpy and furious at the boredom of it all. And I
simply can't stand commuting, the trains are dirty and
useless, the traffic's a nightmare – why can't people get out
of their fucking cars and give me some room. I drive a
Space Cruiser! That demands space! (*Despair, defeat.*) Can't
people see I'm important, can't people see I'm winning. I'm
thin, my make-up's immaculate, my wardrobe is up to the
minute, I read the right magazines, watch the right films,
and I know the right things to say. I even know what post-
ironic means. And, Toolly, can't you put those bloody
binoculars down!

Echo (*to* **Lydia** *and* **Toolly**)   What are you thinking? Sex?
Hot, rampant, reckless sex? Anything you like, anything you
can? Yes, I'm sure that's what you're thinking. Okay, go
with it. Your hair plastered to your head with sweat. The
heat air-drying the spittle of licks, kisses, bites on your neck,
chest, face, stomach, legs, back, arse, groin. Your mouth
licking kissing biting sucking the cock, the cunt that's
nearest, next to you. Slide your cock into my hard calloused
hands, my open salivating mouth, my sisters' slippy, spunk-
filled cunts, my brothers' tight, wet and sweaty, half-greased
arses. Everything dripping, everything sticky and sliding
from someone else's juice.

Toolly (*to* **Lydia**)   You slag. (*They get it on.*)

Echo   'Hard calloused hands.' Hard calloused hands.
Because we work. We farm and labour and build. In this
valley, this beautiful, fertile valley. And our politics? Our
religion? Nobody's ever too keen to ask about that.
Nobody's quite so keen to know about our humanity. Just
the sex. Everybody banging on about the sex. But we
believe everybody here is important. We believe nobody is
more important and nobody is less important. We work
together because we can't survive alone. Self-sufficiency
doesn't work with one. And what we take, we give back and

when we fight and argue and scream we try to ensure the damage is minimal – or at least not permanent. My God is my family, the house, the farm, the animals. I put all my trust and faith in them, because they have no reason to lie to me. I saw my mother single-handedly push a fallen tree trunk off my brother's trapped leg. I saw the rest of my family nurse and comfort both. If that's not God, I don't know what is. I need no other proof – I didn't even need that. Our greatest crime is our lack of hypocrisy. We say what we like and we do what we like. And people visit believing one thing, and stay believing another, or leave in disappointment and the fear of a dose – even though we have regular Aids and VD tests and they don't. So if our reputation damns us, honesty damns us. But nobody wants to hear about that, do they? (*Gets behind* **Toolly**.) Just the sex. Everybody banging on about the sex. And me? I'm not disputing it, it plays a big part, an important part. All bases covered, complete massage, wraparound experience. So what?

Polter   A little judicious press informing. I have friends, contacts. There are children involved. What about tax evasion – not that any of them work but, there must be some money from somewhere. The property's also falling about their ears, environmental health would want to know – they may even be squatters. Social services, bailiffs, Inland Revenue, police naturally. And I'm sure the press could add to the list, add to the outrage. If Toolly won't come to his senses, then the senses will have to come to Toolly. And the queer will have to go.

Toolly   Things are getting desperate, they've had suits crawling all over their property, daily, relentlessly. Echo's sitting tight, thinking it'll pass, it'll blow over. 'They've got nothing,' he says, 'nothing on us, nothing they can get us with.' He's wrong of course. What they've got is his naivety.

Echo   We educate our children because we believe children are important not because education is important. If we sent our children away to be educated, even for one hour, for half a day, we would be honouring the system of education, not honouring our children. I know how to shear a sheep, I know how to grow and harvest food as well as cook it, I know how to divide 3,176 by 14, I know what the capital of Peru is, I know how to spell onomatopoeia – and what it means, I have read the collected works of William Shakespeare, re-enacted some of the good bits with my brothers and sisters for the amusement and entertainment of my family, I can mend a roof, know the principles of solar energy and have helped make a wind turbine. Some day I hope to be a glass-blower. What this place needs is glass.

Lydia   Guilt. Deep-gnawing, erosive guilt. I am not a bad person, just a greedy person. I like comfort, I want comfort, comfort gives me security. Maybe insecurity should be a crime, or an ambition. Those people, I couldn't live with them, couldn't live like them. They have nothing and they have more than me. They make-do-and-mend and they laugh – a lot. The women wear no make-up and the men find them beautiful, their tits are sagging and the men find them beautiful, their legs are hairy, their armpits are hairy, their pubes are like a bush, wild, thick, shapeless and smelling – of sex, female sex, male sex, fresh sex, stale sex. Oh, but they wash, don't get me wrong, they look dirty, but when you get close, when you look at them properly, smell them properly, the smell is clean, the women are clean – as are the men – the smell of sex is strong because sex is strong. The smell of sex is there because I see it there, I smell it there. These women like sex, have sex, want to have sex. These women have sex with their stomachs relaxed and paunchy, their shoulders rounded, their noses running with sweat, their hair tangled, their stretch marks displayed like badges of courage and their cellulite ignored. These women know how to have sex, with men, and with each other. These women know how to be women. They haven't read it in a magazine. These women offered to childmind, offered to educate, offered to look after our children while I went off to look after our bank account. I can no longer plead boredom to escape the house, no longer plead isolation to

justify the hellish commute. I come home in the evenings
and a bowl of oranges strategically placed in a minimalist
chrome kitchen seems to be laughing at me.

Toolly   Echo.

Echo   They've done us on the drugs, usual thing,
cannabis. Moral outrage? I don't think so. They can't touch
us for the poppies, it's not illegal to grow poppies, not our
fault mushrooms just appear in the grass. Maverick owns
the house, owns the land – well, he did, years ago he turned
it over to joint ownership. Tutti does the accounts, she's a
mathematical genius. All our children sat tests. All our
children have been interviewed. We are beginning to worry
about our children, they keep being interviewed.

Toolly   Nobody here is straight, nobody here is gay. No
black, white, right or wrong. To begin with my cock was
burning, to begin with my cock was sore and still Echo let
me carry on, let me persist, let me have him over and over.
His beautiful face and his beautiful body, I wanted to drown
in his arms, I wanted him to drown in mine. This is not
snatched, this is not cottaging, this is not posing and
politicking and protesting/pleading/pretending normality –
this IS normality, part of it. And this is dangerous. Echo,
this is dangerous.

Echo   This isn't dangerous.

Polter   This is an outrage! This goes against everything
that humankind has worked for. This goes against God,
goes against civilisation, against moral decency and
humanity. (*Pointing at* **Echo**.) You disgust me, you are
depraved. You have opted out of the system, chosen to
wallow around in a cesspit of your own making and you ask
for acceptance. What have you done? What have you done
for mankind? Except indulged your own selfish pursuits.
What do you know about work? About sacrifice and duty?
About doing the decent thing, the right thing, obeying the
law, following rules, maintaining society, containing society?
Where the hell do you think we'd be if everybody was like

you? Stumbling over the rubble of anarchy, chaos and lawlessness. You are lower than human, lower than an animal, you make me sick.

Echo (*to* **Polter**)   Fancy a fuck?

Toolly   Echo, don't.

Echo (*to* **Polter**)   Come on, you know you want to, it's why you're here. It's why everybody's here, why everybody comes, we're well known, we're famous, thanks to you. We're plastered across every newspaper, every television and radio report, they're doing in-depth one-hour specials on us – with dramatic reconstruction by desperate-to-work actors. So come on, let's fuck, it's what you want, what you expect of me, it's what you're obsessed with – get your dick out, stick it somewhere, fuck, come on, I want a fuck, I want to fuck you!

Polter   You're dead!

Echo   I know.

Toolly   You shouldn't have done that, Echo.

Echo   I know that too.

Lydia   They want to take the children. Social services are there with the police. Well 'there' – they can't get in, can't get close. The press and media are closer, they've got a bird's-eye view. Echo and the family have barricaded themselves in, there's a stand-off, somebody said there's a shotgun, I never saw a shotgun but . . . this is farming territory. They're talking about sexual abuse, they're talking about satanic ritual – I've never met a nicer bunch of well-rounded kids. Scruffy, yes. Precocious, yes. A little bit wild, yes. Sexually abused, no. I don't think so.

Polter   You've got to get away from here, you've got to leave. It's all going to go sky-high and I don't want the media shoving cameras in your faces when it does.

Toolly   You're going to destroy these people's lives, break up their community because I'm gay?

Polter   You're not gay, Toolly, you've been corrupted. You've been offered an alternative, a chance to think. That's got to be stopped.

Echo   We do not abuse our children. We love our children, we spend more time with them than you do, we don't see them as an interruption, a hindrance, a burden or a nuisance.

Toolly   You may not have sex with them, but you have sex in front of them, Echo, I've seen it.

Echo   You've seen nothing, you've only thought you've seen it because you expect to see it. Would Lydia trust us? Would Lydia trust your children to us? I don't think so. You are a hypocrite, Toolly. Not even Polter is as hypocritical as you. Our children are behind walls when we fuck, just the same as your children are. If a child should happen to walk in while we're fucking . . . well . . . I don't know, Toolly, what do you do? Cover the erection and pretend you're playing wrestling?

Toolly   If social services think your children are at risk . . .

Echo   If social services think our children are at risk they would have done something years ago, before their morale was ground down and the word 'scapegoat' was thrown. They've been round before, we're well known in the area, they know us, we know them. We've lived here years, way before you came. I was born here, this is all I know. But, Toolly, maybe the media want the children to be at risk, maybe Polter wants the children to be at risk. Maybe the press and your uncle are prepared to sacrifice our children, sacrifice us, because of you. Because you are a blot on your uncle's copybook, you are an embarrassment, you can't be explained. You've had it all, you've got it all and yet our lifestyle appeals. Why are you still living here, Toolly? Why haven't you moved?

No answer from **Toolly**.

Lydia   You can't go along with this, Toolly, you can't
agree. Our children have played with their children. We've
bought food that they've grown, we've eaten with them.
You know they're not bad people.

Toolly   And I know you can't live in poverty, Lydia, so
shut up.

Lydia   I got bored with the Porsche years ago. So why are
we still living here, Toolly? Why haven't we moved?

Echo   Toolly's got a Porsche but he hardly ever drives it
any more. He drove me once, into town. I laughed my head
off but I was terrified – it's not the same as being in the back
of a police van, you can see out and I thought the trees were
going to hit us. In town I couldn't get over the shops, so
many shops, so many things to buy, so many people buying
things. I don't know how they choose. I couldn't choose, I
didn't know what to buy, I didn't know what I needed.
Then I realised I needed everything, so I still didn't know
what to choose. In the end I just got a headache and an
overwhelming urge to scream so Toolly drove me home. I
don't understand it, I can't live in it, I don't want to need
everything. I don't want them to take our children away and
teach them to need everything. They want to break us up,
destroy what we've got. Lydia says we've got nothing, so I
suppose nothing is what they're going to destroy.

Polter   Your aunt and I brought you up.

Toolly   Polter brought me up.

Polter   We educated you.

Toolly   They educated me.

Polter   Sex isn't success.

Toolly   I can live without Echo.

Polter   Appearance is everything.

Toolly   I can't live without Polter.

Polter   So why are you still living here, Toolly? Why haven't you moved?

Lydia   I can't manage I can't cope. We sacked the nanny, she couldn't even speak English. I spend all day on the farm chatting and working with friends, the kids eat properly, we feed them organic. Have you see what's in the freezer? Home-grown. Everything! I could stay at home, bring them up properly, collectively. And I simply couldn't stand commuting, the trains were dirty and useless, the traffic a nightmare – why can't people get out of their fucking cars and give themselves some room. (*Despair, defeat.*) I wanted people to see that I was important, I wanted people to see me winning. I was thin – for people to see. My make-up was immaculate – for people to see. My wardrobe was up to the minute – for people to see. I read the right magazines, for approval. Watched the right films, for approval. And I knew the right things to say, for approval. I even knew what post-ironic meant, so that people could watch me laugh at myself. I looked at myself through binoculars, worrying about what other people saw. ECHO!

Toolly *and* **Polter** *hit her down.*

Toolly   No!

Polter   You've been corrupted. You've been offered an alternative, a chance to think.

Toolly   That's got to be stopped.

Lydia (*getting up*)   They feed themselves, clothe themselves, look after their own. They live quietly, privately, in their beautiful little valley. They've never harmed anyone, never tried to recruit or convert. They have sex. Pathetic. All this because they have sex. Sex without guilt. Sex without control.

Toolly *and* **Polter** *push her down.*

Lydia (*getting up again*)   And we're frightened of putting a hair out of place, frightened of people laughing. We have to be on top, better than the rest. I didn't like my life, I was perfecting my life, making it better, and better and better. Now I've found a way. Echo!

Toolly *and* **Polter** *push her down.*

Lydia (*getting up*)   It's what I want. What you want too. You love him, Toolly. Echo!

Toolly (*pushing her down*)   I can't love Echo, I'm not allowed to love Echo, Echo's losing, he's too powerful to be controlled and small enough to be swamped. Echo's dead.

Lydia *gets up.*

Toolly   If you go with Echo, the kids stay with me.

Lydia *freezes halfway up.*

Echo   Why are you doing this?

Polter   You are not getting Toolly's power.

Echo   I don't want it.

Polter   But he's giving it away, letting it slip, and I cannot allow him to give away my power, my influence, my way of life.

Echo   You're losing control.

Polter   He was almost a son, he was the nearest thing to a son.

Echo   You're losing.

Polter   I'm not losing, I'm growing. Growing, thriving, and winning. I'm winning. Who are you the son of? Who are you a father to? Who do you have control over? Nobody. You're dead.

Pause.

Echo Did you know that the penis is not just an exterior organ? It continues deep inside the body, running parallel and adjacent to the anal canal. Some day I hoped to be a glass-blower. What this place needs is glass.

A giant, cosmic, pyrotechnic explosion. Something never before achieved in the history of British, penniless, tatty, gaffer-taped theatre.

Polter Straw bales, candles and cheap, shoddy Calor gas heaters. Tragic. It was the children I felt most sorry for.

Toolly (*questioning*) Calor gas heaters? They didn't have Calor gas heaters.

Polter (*shrugs*) These things happen.

Pause.

Polter What you going to say?

Toolly Nothing.

Polter What you going to say?

Toolly It was necessary.

Polter What you going to say?

Toolly It was meant, it was holy, it was righteous.

Polter *nods.*

Polter Now, let's go and feed the Dobermanns. Oh, by the way, did I tell you your aunt is finally pregnant?

Lydia (*still frozen*) ECHO!

Polter *and* **Toolly** *push her down.*

Printed in the USA
CPSIA information can be obtained
at www.ICGtesting.com
LVHW041058171024
794057LV00001B/145

9 780413 761804